The Cambridge Manuals of Science and
Literature

THE BALLAD IN LITERATURE

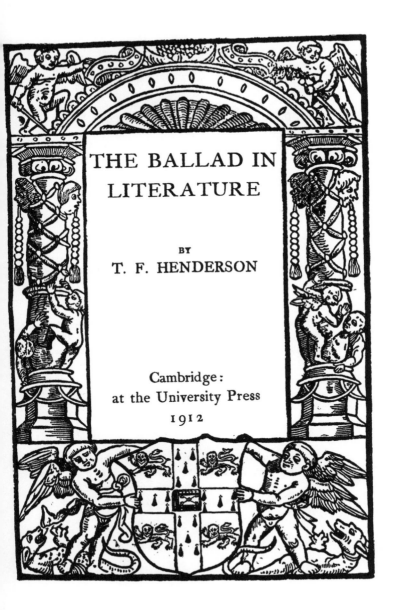

THE BALLAD IN LITERATURE

BY

T. F. HENDERSON

Cambridge:
at the University Press
1912

CAMBRIDGE UNIVERSITY PRESS
Cambridge, New York, Melbourne, Madrid, Cape Town,
Singapore, São Paulo, Delhi, Tokyo, Mexico City

Cambridge University Press
The Edinburgh Building, Cambridge CB2 8RU, UK

Published in the United States of America by Cambridge University Press, New York

www.cambridge.org
Information on this title: www.cambridge.org/9781107605770

First published 1912
First paperback edition 2011

A catalogue record for this publication is available from the British Library

ISBN 978-1-107-60577-0 Paperback

*With the exception of the coat of arms at
the foot, the design on the title page is a
reproduction of one used by the earliest known
Cambridge printer, John Siberch, 1521*

PREFACE

WITHIN recent years much has been done in the accumulation of data towards the explication of that, in some respects, mysterious kind of verse, known in England as the traditional ballad. In different countries specimens have been collected and published in great abundance, and much editorial learning has been expended in illustrative exposition and comment. Its distinctive characteristics—so far as they are preserved in surviving tradition, and comparatively late MS. and printed examples— have thus been now as fully disclosed as probably they will ever be.

In regard to its genesis, its development and the character of its authorship, we are met, at the outset, with the difficulty of a lack of direct evidence. There is no record as to how this species of verse originated, or as to how it found its way into different countries. Here we have nothing to guide us but vague incidental statements and inferences founded on a variety of considerations which are still, more or less, subjects of dispute. No very early authentic specimens of the ballad survive. All have been in some degree modified by tradition ; and even the antiquity of the earliest surviving ballads, the historical as well as the non-historical, can be determined only approximately.

Still the minute study of other forms of early verse, and the very comprehensive knowledge we now possess of the literary characteristics and themes of the surviving ballad versions of different nations, have tended to dissipate various erroneous preconceptions, and, on several important points, have supplied the means of more than plausible conjecture ; and comparison and criticism may still further help to clear up difficulties, and bring about a more general agreement of opinion.

The similarities and dissimilitudes between the ballads of different countries are, in varied ways, interesting and suggestive, and afford scope for more extended and minute discussion than was possible within the limits of this volume. The most pregnant revelation is the apparent predominance of France, both in shaping, at least indirectly, the ballad as we now know it, and in supplying ballad themes. This predominance extends not merely, as we might expect, to Britain, or to Northern Italy and Northern Spain,

but very specially, and more than to Germany, to
Denmark, whether the predominance there be direct
or indirect.   This fact alone helps to dissipate some
of the mystery attaching to the origin of the ballad,
and although there is still a good deal that is in-
explicable in regard to its beginnings or creation,
and the extension of its vogue in different countries,
further light on the subject may yet be available.

The study of folklore has supplied much interesting
information bearing on ballad themes ; but folklore,
if one of the most fascinating, is perhaps one of the
most deceptive forms of learning.   It is the happy
hunting ground for the sciolist.   It is fruitful in
fallacies for the rash theoriser ; and it can hardly be
affirmed that caution has been prominent in folklore
theorizing about the ballad.

On the controversial points touched on in this
volume, I have sought to state the pros and cons as
fairly as I could.   I have done my best to appreciate
the views and arguments of those from whom I in
any way differ.   In most instances of importance
their opinions are quoted in their own words ; and if
I have, in any way, misinterpreted them, it is not
from lack of effort, but lack of ability, to understand
them.

The numbers attached in brackets to individual ballads refer to their sequence in Child's *English and Scottish Ballads*, 1882-98.   This must ever remain the standard collection of British ballad versions ; and its careful and minute illustrations, from folklore, romances, tales, and the ballad versions of other countries, are beyond praise.

T. F. H.

December 15th, 1911.

CONTENTS

THE
BALLAD IN LITERATURE

CHAPTER I

THE LITERARY FORM, CHARACTER AND SOURCES OF THE BALLAD

DANCE and music have an almost inseparable connection; and poetry has a close association with both. If the Darwinian hypothesis of man's origin be accepted, dancing of a kind most probably preceded definite articulate speech and anything that could properly be termed music. In the primeval world of man it may well have been associated with some sort of rude chant, before instrumental music—except such sounds as those of the tom-tom—was attempted; and whether song, or the germs of poetry, originally existed apart from the dance, rude chants have been used as dance music, and as a means of arousing dancing fervour, by tribes in what is now deemed a very primitive condition of civilization. Even in the early centuries of the Christian era, the deeds of heroes and the victories of great warriors were amongst European

A

peoples celebrated in dance songs, though contemporary with these dance songs were the *chansons de geste*, composed by the minstrel harper and sung in the tents of the warrior chiefs or in the halls of the great lords. Minstrels of a ruder kind as well as female dancers were also accustomed to accompany the army for the special delectation of the common soldiers, as is mentioned by Ethelred of the army of David II. of Scotland, at the battle of the Standard in 1138 ; and it was apparently to some such camp followers that we owe the naïve mocking chant preserved by Fabyan, celebrating the Scottish victory at Bannockburn :—

> " Maydens of Englonde, sore may ye morne,
>   For your lemmans ye have lostë at Bannockisborne !
>   With heue a lowe.
>   What wenyth the Kynge of Englonde
>   So soone to have wonne Scotland :
>   With rumby lowe."

which song, we are told by Fabyan, " was after many dayes sungyn in dances, in carolles of ye maydens and mynstrellys of Scotlande."

The *carole* was the ancient circular dance with joined hands, accompanied by a song and sometimes instrumental music. The oldest form of the *carole* was, like that celebrating Bannockburn, in couplets sung by the chief singer, the chorus of dancers repeating the refrain. Originally the refrain, as in the case of the Bannockburn song, was merely imitative of some kind of action, or of the sound of a musical instrument. Later they were exclamatory, and ultimately they formed a line or two lines riming together. The ballad or *ballada*, derived originally from the southern Italian *ballare*, to dance — a word probably of Greek origin — was originally used in Italy in the same general sense as the *carole* in France. Dante assigns it a lower place than the song proper and the sonnet on account of its dependence on the aid of the dancers ; but as the *ballete* in France, the *ballada* in Provence, the *ballata*, *ballatetta* and *ballatina* in Italy, it was later used to signify a form of the *carole*, of which there were also various modifications, created by the introduction of an additional rhyme. The word *ballade* was thus ultimately employed by French poets to signify an artfully constructed lyric of three rhymes — *ab*, *ab*, *bc*, *bc*, including a refrain, the rhymes being identical throughout the three stanzas—and an envoy of four lines rhyming with the latter half of the octave. The *rondet*, the *virelai*, the *rondel* and the *rondeau* were also, originally, additional varieties of the *carole*. On these various forms of verse the dance has left its impress. It has had an important share in shaping the metrical forms of poetry, just as its influence has done much to determine the metre or rhythm of music. But in Europe generally, lyrism has become dissociated from the dance, just as many forms of music have become independent of it or of song, or of both ; though there are survivals of the old connection in certain communities and in certain species of comic songs and portions of comic opera.

Of this old world of dance songs, now known to us mainly by faint and vague records and by imperfect examples and fragmentary remains of its verse, there is still a kind of surviving microcosm— or rather a partial and modified renascence—in the Faroe Isles. There we have the double anomaly of a lack of instrumental music—or any trace of its existence—and the extraordinary predominance of the dance song. Although songs are sung on certain occasions without the accompaniment of the dance, the motions of the dancers are inspired and regulated not by instrumental music but by song ; and the mediæval world of song and dance has in quite a wondrous fashion been partially preserved. Another striking thing is that the dance themes of the Faroe dance songs are derived from foreign sources, chiefly Norwegian and Icelandic, a favourite subject being that of the hero Sigurd. The prevailing form of dance is the old circle dance of France and of ancient Greece ; but the songs do not resemble the old French *caroles*; they are mainly lyric-epic. In addition to the old ballads of native origin, but derived mainly from Icelandic stories or legends, various Danish ballads in the Danish language, facetious or satirical songs and modern Norwegian and Danish songs are also included; while the fisher people have very rude dance songs of their own creation. None of the native Faroe ballads can be older than the fourteenth century : most are later ; and the introduction of the Danish ballads is supposed to have begun in the sixteenth century. Other forms of the dance are had recourse to on special occasions, and there are also various kinds of dance plays. After the marriage feast the newly-married couple and the guests, with the pastor in his robes, dance a solemn dance, singing a nuptial song of a sacred character ; and then follows a kind of saturnalia of feasting, singing and dancing, continued until the following morning and resumed again next day.

According to its derivation, the term ballad might apply to any of the Faroe forms of dance song ; but the oldest forms of verse known in England as ballads are the lyric-epics, known in Spain as *romances*, in Germany as *volkslieder*, in Scandinavia as *folkeviser*, in Brittany as *gwerzou*, and included, without specific title, amongst the popular songs of France, Catalonia, Provence, North

Italy, etc. From a comparatively early period political songs—including those of a satirical character—were in England usually termed ballads ; and since a good many Danish ballads deal with subjects of contemporary interest, it may be that there were old English ballads now lost which did so. The old Scots makaris wrote also a kind of narrative poem or song, termed a ballad, mostly, but not always, relating love experiences. A fine example is the *Robene and Makeyne* of Henryson, in the ballad stave of *Chevy Chase*. So is the anonymous poem, *The Mourning Maiden*, possibly, under the name *the levis greene*, referred to as a dance in *The Complaynt of Scotland* (c. 1548). Non-amatory specimens are *Allan-a-Maut*—the oldest of the *John Barleycorn* songs or ballads—and *The Ballad of Kynd Kittok* in the alliterative stave of the old romances. These latter look like a kind of parody of the serious lyric-epic, now known to us as the traditional ballad. This kind of ballad for its full effectiveness as a song or recital called in originally the aid of a chorus and, probably, of the dance. Its refrain nearly everywhere was originally that of the simpler French *carole*, a form especially suitable for this kind of narrative song. Its essential function is to tell a tale—not usually, as in the case of the *fabliau*, with a view to awaken mirth, though at a later period mirth and satire adopted the old ballad forms—but to stir the deeper and more serious emotions, wonder, terror, sorrow, exultation. A species of the ballad is, also, somewhat allied to the old *chanson de geste*. Many Danish ballads are a kind of revival in a new form of the old heroic lays; the short episodic romances of Spain in eight-syllabled assonants are founded directly on the longer *cantares de gesta*; in the fifteenth and six-teenth century ballads of France and Northern Italy, contemporary events are also represented; and in Britain the Robin Hood ballads, the later Border ballads and other historical or semi-historical ballads have a certain similarity in tone to the older historic verse of the early minstrels. But while the scope of the ballad theme is much wider than that of the *chanson de geste*, it differs from purely epic verse in that, while it is confined to a single episode, it is concerned with the thing done or the event that happened rather than with the personality or personalities. Its aim, whether recited or sung, or sung and danced, is to tell a good story about anybody or anything, no matter what or whom. The personalities might almost be labelled in algebraic fashion; they are there mainly to develop a dramatic situation, to bring about an affecting dramatic climax. To develop the situation the device of the riddle is sometimes employed, just as Shakespeare in *The Merchant of Venice* employs the device of the Caskets ; but the ballad is not to be confounded with what are affirmed to be improvised riddle songs. Nor can mere coronachs or lyke-wake dirges be properly termed ballads ; for they have no tale to tell.

While the ballad lacks the measured rhetoric, the stately movement and pomp of epic verse, this is no sufficient reason for assigning it a special artistic inferiority. Its aim and method are different ; and the goodness or badness of art is not a matter of special aims and methods, but of the successful or non-successful application of a certain method to the accomplishment of a particular aim. The aim of the ballad was more restricted than that of epic verse, and its method more complex and more dramatic. It sought to impress by the vivid representation of a single event, to bring home to the hearer its wonder, its pathos, its fatefulness, or its horror. It did so aided by music, instrumental often as well as vocal, and it often added to the emotional impression by the device of the refrain sung by a chorus, and at one time probably danced as well as sung. Abstractly, there is no reason why verse with such an aim should be artistically inferior to the old epic verse, however less stately it might be—that it should be less poetical and more nearly allied to doggerel. This would depend on the poetic endowment and artistic efficiency or inefficiency of the balladist; and the fact that doggerel has now largely triumphed in many traditional ballads is of course no proof that it was always there. The opinion of Professor Child, gathered from various statements in his ballad introductions, as summed up by Mr W. M. Hart—*Publications of the Modern Language Association of America* for 1906—is that the ballad is "at its best when it is early caught and fixed in print"; and since almost none of the earlier ballads have been so caught until centuries after they were first sung, we may fairly conclude that originally these early ballads were much superior to such mutilated and variegated specimens as now, for the most part, are all that we have to represent them. True, some, as we shall find, more than hint that the genuine ballad of tradition is, like good wine, mellowed rather than corrupted by age; but great as may have been the respect of Professor Child for folk tradition, he did not propose to endow it with such wonderful gifts as the more extreme communalists are disposed to claim for it.

The earliest Danish MSS. date from 1550; and there are no early MS. versions for Italian, French, Spanish or other continental ballads. In English a rhymed account in couplets of the treachery of Judas (23), classed by Professor Child as a ballad, is found in a thirteenth century manuscript in Trinity College, Cambridge. However it may be classed, it is not a notable production ; but it shows no signs of debasement either in language or rhyme. Similar remarks apply to *St Stephen and Herod* (22), in .the Sloane MS., supposed to be in a hand-writing of the time of Henry VI. *Riddles Wisely Expounded* (1), in the Rawlinson MS. of 1450, if rather silly, is hardly debased, certainly not so much so as the black-letter variation with its "Lay the bent to the bonny broom," and its "La La la la la," etc., nor as the Motherwell traditional version—inspired without doubt by the black-letter—with its "Sing the Cather banks, the bonnie brume" and its "And ye may beguile a young maid sune."

The original of a *Thomas Rhymer* ballad (37) is evidently to be found in a fragmentary portion of the MS. romance of *Thomas of Erceldoune*, dating from about the beginning of the fifteenth century, but it is hardly possible to credit that the so-called traditional ballad is other than a comparatively modern concoction from the romance : that the romance fragment, which evidently was never danced, should be transformed into its later ballad shape by the gradual processes of folk tradition, will appear to most people a plain impossibility, though it has been pronounced "an entirely popular ballad as to style,"

The *Gest of Robin Hood*, which is little more than a collection of ballads about that otherwise unknown outlaw, was in print early in the sixteenth century; and some of the best of the Robin Hood ballads are found in MSS. of the previous century. *Robin Hood and the Monk* (119), of about 1450, is notable for its wonderful opening stanzas, which, in a less perfect and more condensed form, begin *Robin Hood and the Potter* (121), of the Cambridge MS. of about 1500, and *Robin and Guy of Gisborne* (118), of the Percy folio MS. of about 1650 :—

> " In somer when the shawes be sheyne,
>   And leves be large and long,
> Hit is full mery in feyre foreste
>   To here the foulys song :
>
> To se the dere draw to the dale,
>   And leve the hilles hee,
> And shadow he i' the leves grene
>   Vndr the grene-wode tre."

It would be impossible to better these old-world stanzas by any form of amendment ; not only are they beyond artistic reproach ; they attain their purpose with exquisite felicity.

A much shorter ballad, *Robyn and Gandeleyn* (115), in an MS. of about 1450, is quite different in style from the general Robin Hood ballads.   It possesses an effective refrain, " Robyn lyeth in grene wode bowndyn," is more antique in its diction, is here and there alliterative, and in the closing stanzas shows what Professor Gummere calls "incremental repetition," meant to emphasize what may be termed the climax of the narrative. Repetition of a faint character also occurs in the seventh and eighth stanzas. It is an admirable ballad alike in conception, method and, but for some imperfect rhymes, execution : the fortunate achievement of no mean poetic artist. The *Sir Andrew Barton* (167) version of the sixteenth century and that in the Percy MS. represent a much lower style of ballad art; but it might be rash to affirm that the original *Sir Andrew Barton* was inferior to *Robyn and Gandeleyn*.

The copy of *The Hunting of the Cheviot* (162)—which ballad is mentioned in *The Complaynt of Scotland* as one of the " sangis of natural music of the antiquitee "—in the Ashmole MS. (*c.* 1510) is plainly a deteriorated version of one originally of some artistic accomplishment. It is sixtyeight stanzas long in quatrains of alternate rhymes sometimes extending into an octave :—

> " The dryvars thorowe the wood went
>   for to reas the dear ;
> Bomen byckarte vppone the bent
>   wt ther browd aros cleare :

Then the wyld thorowe the wood went
  on eury sydë shear :
Greahonds thorowe the grevis glent
  for to kyll thear dear."

A Memorable Song on the Unhappy Hunting in Chevy Chase is a free rendering in black-letter gibberish of the older version. An English version, also in quatrains of alternate rhymes, of the analogous *Battle of Otterbourne* (161), in the Cottonian and Harleian MSS. (*c.* 1550), is spirited and vivid, but much ruder in expression and rhyme than the *Hunting of the Cheviot.* The first stanza of this ballad is nearly identical with that quoted by Hume of Godscroft (1560-1630) as commencing a Scots song " made of Otterborne," which, he says, narrates the occasion and incidents of the battle " almost as in authentic history " ; but if this ballad now in any form exists, which is more than doubtful, it does so only in very late tradition.

The Percy folio MS. (*c.* 1650) is of considerable account as a source of ballad versions. Though its various specimens of the ballad differ greatly in literary worth, it supplies interesting evidence both in regard to later traditional deteriorations and to Percy's methods of amendment and transformation ; but besides that it is comparatively late, its value is impaired by the fact that for over a century a certain species of transmission by printed versions had been in operation. Many of the Percy folio versions smack of the broadside ; there are even broadsides that closely resemble some of them in tenor and style ; and, as a rule, broadsides are merely vulgar, sometimes facetiously vulgar, travesties of the old ballad.

The existence of broadside versions also largely discounts the antique worth—whatever otherwise it might be—of traditional versions obtained in the eighteenth and nineteenth centuries. Even when these versions are traditional in the sense of not being retouched by the collector, they are more often than not merely a traditional rendering of a broadside or chap-book version of an old ballad. In many cases this is only too evident ; but these delusive traditional versions are much more common than can be directly proved, for the simple reason that broadside and stall copies are the most perishable of all forms of literature. Apart from indirect evidence of particular broadsides having perished, the mere fact that only single specimens of some, and only a very few specimens of many, are known to survive, is a significant sign of the previous existence of a large number of which we now know nothing. In the British Museum there is even a thick volume of white-letter sheets of the eighteenth century, not known to exist apart from the volume which now contains them, and preserving Scottish songs, many of them rather free in expression, and Scottish ballad versions not, to my knowledge, preserved elsewhere. But even when the ballad has escaped the transmogrification of the broadside artist, the traditional version usually represents a very blurred and deteriorated form of any possible original. Many exist only in fragments, or have got almost hopelessly mixed up with each other ; catchwords, phrases, isolated stanzas have also become commonplaces scattered promiscuously about in different versions ; rhyme has often almost vanished, sometimes even assonance, and such rhyme or assonance as survives is, in many cases, a source of pain rather than of pleasure to the ear.

In Denmark, owing partly to the care of the Danish ladies who copied them, and often to the higher character of the tradition as well as to other causes, there is a general superiority in ballad versions over those of any other country. Here we have more frequent glimpses of the excellent character of the ancient ballad art. As in France and Italy, the refrain appears more frequently than in British and German ballads. Though, as as is usual in ballads, it is in the simpler form of the *carole*, there are considerable varieties. Sometimes it is the ancient imitative refrain, used in English and Scottish versions of black-letter derivation in a

heterogeneous and meaningless fashion. Occasionally, in the case of couplets, it is a kind of echo by
the chorus of what the chief singer had sung : a
repetition of the latter half of the first line and the
whole of the second ; and it is easy to understand
how effective this might be in the case of the more
weird and tragic ballads.   Often the refrain is
apposite to the tenor of the ballad, and sometimes it
condenses its sentiment, its wild passion or its pathos
with peculiar power.   When the refrain is of this
variety, the ballad itself is almost inevitably of a
superior kind, or originally has been so ; but the
meaningless refrain, or the refrain introduced
malapropos may be as old as the other.   Doubtless,
as in all other forms of verse, there were balladists
who were artists and poets, and balladists who were
not ;   and whatever the impersonality or com-
munality of ballads may mean, it cannot surely
imply that ballads were all originally of the same
level of excellence.

Various Danish ballads, like several of the English
and Scottish ballads, have the same refrain ;   and
different versions of the same ballad have different
refrains.   In the Faroes, the refrain sung by the
chorus of dancers is of considerable length, of somewhat irregular form, and generally of a lyric character.   Few Faroe ballads have a special refrain
of their own ; the same refrain with its own special

refrain melody does duty for a considerable number of ballads.

In couplets, more common in Danish than in English ballads, the refrain occurs at the end of each line; in quatrains, more common in English than Danish ballads, it occurs at the close of the verse. German ballads lack interior refrains. In the French and Italian ballads assonance is frequently used, the verse consisting, in this case, either of two or three lines—never more—sometimes of as many as sixteen syllables. The refrain may be either between the lines or at the end of the verse. The octosyllabic quatrain of two rhymes is also common; and there are various other modifications of the rhymed quatrain. The later British ballads generally lack the refrain. Couplets with interior refrains are in Danish and British ballads mostly octosyllabic, but the single rhyme verse of four lines is virtually in couplets, though the line is broken up by a natural pause in the rhythm. The usual forms are the eight and six and eight and seven varieties, but there are several others. Other verse forms are also found, and their variety may have been greater than is now known, for later tradition, the tradition favoured by the folkists, that of the nurse, the woolspinner, the weaver, the peasant, and so forth, is necessarily limited by its peculiar preferences, and, apparently, is capable of trans-

B

mitting only very rugged examples of verse, and those in its simpler forms.

In addition to deterioration by recital, tradition and black- and white-letter travesty, English and Scottish ballads have often been made to undergo processes of change by the pens of collectors and, more especially, collecting editors. Several Scottish ballads were included in Allan Ramsay's *Evergreen*, 1724, and his *Tea Table Miscellany*, four volumes, 1724-32 ; and, in most cases, it is hard to tell how much these versions owe to his poetic fancy. Bishop Percy, who published his *Reliques of Ancient Poetry* in 1765, " was accustomed," to use the words of Sir Walter Scott, " to restore the ancient ballad by throwing in touches of poetry, so adapted to its tone and tenor as to assimilate with the original structure, and impress one who considered the subject as being coeval with the rest of the piece." Percy himself states that he had " endeavoured to be as faithful " to his copy " as the imperfect state of his materials could admit " ; but that he could not think of scrupulous adherence to many of the wretched readings, " when by a few slight corrections or additions, a most beautiful or interesting sense hath started forth, and this so naturally and easily that the Editor could seldom prevail on himself to indulge the vanity of making a formal claim to the improvement." This is expressed so naïvely as almost to disarm criticism and dissipate curiosity ; but the publication of the Percy folio MS. in 1867-8, and discoveries of other ballad versions, have revealed that the bishop has been far too modest in stating the extent and character of his amendments. It is manifest that he possessed a quite exceptional aptitude for imitating the old ballad manner in such a way as immensely to improve the literary form of the versions that came into his hands, and yet retain a more than passable semblance of the ancient ballad style. That he was not endowed with the peculiar transforming power of Burns was here to his advantage : the genius of Burns is hardly to be hidden in any amendment that he made. Its exceptional excellence is its undoing. Nor could Sir Walter Scott sufficiently restrain the individuality of his muse in many of his amendments ; but Percy just possessed the amount of poetic skill necessary to accomplish a feasible piece of patchwork.

In the *Reliques*, Percy did not confine himself to what is termed the traditional ballad. It contains many signed pieces, some by well-known poets, and includes comparatively modern as well as ancient verse, and songs and other forms of verse as well as ballads. His aim was literary rather than antiquarian ; and apart from pecuniary considerations—though these were evidently not overlooked—propagandist rather than critical. It was avowedly to make known the antique poetic charm of the old popular verse, to stimulate an interest in it as poetry ; and that being so, he inserted no ballad in a fragmentary fashion, and allowed no more than traces of literary debasement to appear in any versions that he published. The success of the book was immediate, and its effect much greater than he could have anticipated in his wildest dreams. Its vogue was more than a popular one. It assisted to create the German romantic movement, and was the precursor of the modern ballad art of the great poets of the golden age of German literature. In Britain the most conspicuously noteworthy of its consequences was the impression which, many years after its publication, it produced on young Walter Scott, and the zeal with which it inspired him for the collection of old ballads. Later, Scott came also under the spell of the German romantic movement which the *Reliques* had a share in creating, and he in his turn, and his great contemporary Byron, were, in the early nineteenth century, to give a new impetus to romanticism throughout Europe.

So far as mere ballad lore was concerned, the influence of Scott's *Border Minstrelsy*, the first edition of which appeared in 1801, was much greater

than that of Percy's *Reliques*, except as regards
Germany, previously inspired by Percy. As was
natural, the influence of the *Minstrelsy* manifested
itself more immediately in Scotland than in
England; and as a matter of fact the chief
traditionary versions of British ballads are those
obtained by Scottish collectors. Scott had some
predecessors. In 1769 the Edinburgh clerk, David
Herd, published anonymously *Ancient and Modern
Scottish Songs*, an enlarged edition appearing in 1776.
A few versions of old ballads were included in
the volumes. Herd was an indefatigable collector,
and he manifested the exceptional merit of adding
nothing to the versions, either to help the grammar
or rhyme or to complete the song or ballad. He
was incapable of writing verse, and he was more
interested in collecting than in book-making. Some
old ballads were also included in Pinkerton's
Scottish Ballads (1783), in Ritson's *Ancient Songs*
(1790), and in Johnson's *Scots Musical Museum*
(1787-1803), several ballad versions being sent to it
by Burns. But the *Border Minstrelsy* was, as
regards ballads proper, a much more important
work, both for its versions and its annotations,
than any of its predecessors, including the *Reliques*.
Though several pieces were inserted that have no
claim to be termed ballads, the number printed for
the first time, that properly came under that name,

was greater ; and various others not easily accessible were also reprinted.

Scott's method of dealing with his versions differed somewhat from that of Percy. He succeeded in collecting several, sometimes a good many, versions of the same ballad ; and from the best stanzas, or half stanazs, or lines of these several versions, he compiled a new version of his own, rectifying here and there both the expression and the rhyme, piecing out defective stanzas by lines of his own, and not unfrequently constructing new stanzas in order to, as he expressed it, complete the sense. Often the temptation to accomplish a complete ballad, joined to the desire to do justice at once to the exploits of his ancestors and the verses of their bards, led him to indulge in such liberties with the versions he obtained as to create rather misleading ideas of their literary worth. Whatever the poetic merit of the ancient original might be, it was hardly that sometimes conspicuously manifested in many of the stanzas published by Scott. In his case we have, however, the advantage of knowing the character of the liberties he took with many of the versions he received, for they are nearly all preserved at Abbotsford. In the case of later editors, such as Jamieson, Motherwell, and so forth, our knowledge is less definite, though it is plain that they were under the delusion

that it was specially meritorious to discover a
version which differed, however absurdly, from any
previously published, and that they had theories
about the antiquity and value of country tradition and the nature of ballad completeness, which
tended to lead them wildly astray. The same
remark applies to several collectors who aided Scott,
and while the northern collector Buchan is nearly
always quite beyond consideration, many of the
versions recited or written out by Mrs Brown of
Falkland, who vies with Buchan in voluminousness,
are far from being homogeneous, though others
have quite a traceable connection with broadside
copies.

Yet in some way or other, if by revision, by
revision of which we know nothing, and, in any
case, not by popular tradition, whether by a higher
tradition or not, a few ballad versions of great, of
almost supreme, merit survive. If largely amended,
they have been amended with quite wonderful
skill, and if mainly original they must have been
the work of no mean balladists, balladists of quite
a different order of merit from collective village
communities. The Herd version of the *Wee Wee
Man*, derived from the romance, will, for example,
be recognised by any one who knows the difference
between the old vernacular Scots of the educated
classes and that of the nurse, the weaver, or shepherd,

as altogether superior in its language to the average traditional ballad. Not only so, but it is in almost every respect—in conception as well as execution— an admirable piece of balladry. It could not have passed through the hands of Burns, for it was published by Herd in 1776, when Burns was merely a lad of seventeen ; but if late emendation has been done, it has been effected with quite exceptional skill. The version in Caw's *Museum* is very similar to the Herd ; but the traditional versions printed by Child only serve to illustrate to what depths of prosy and vulgar commonplace a fine ballad may sink, after a few years' subjection to the standards of popular taste. Here is the last stanza of the Herd version :—

> " When we came to the stairfoot
>   Ladies were dancing, jimp and sma ;
>   But in the twinkling of an eye
>   My wee, wee man was clean awa."

And here is what this came to be in popular Aberdeen tradition, as recorded in the Kinloch MSS. of 1826, and after :—

> " There were pipers playing on ilka stair
>   And ladies dancing in ilka ha' ;
>   But before we could have said what was that
>   The house and wee manie was awa."

But a much more striking specimen of balladry,

real or imitative, is *Edward* (13).   It was sent to
Percy by Sir David Dalrymple, Lord Hailes ; and
Percy, but for the absurd " z " changes, must have
printed it very much as he got it, because, for one
thing, it is a quite admirable example of the non-
vulgarised Scots of the seventeenth and later
centuries ; and Percy did not know Scots.   Yet
Professor Child tells us that it is "not only unim-
peachable, but has ever been regarded as one of the
noblest specimens of the popular ballad " ; and
Professor Gummere thinks that it can owe its
concentrated tragic force to nothing else than the
shaping genius of folk tradition.   The verdicts of
both professors seem to be based on an imperfect
acquaintance with the niceties of the Scots dialect ;
at anyrate they indicate no appreciation of the
ballad's utter linguistic superiority to the average
Scottish traditional ballad versions ; but even so,
the debased Motherwell version of this ballad, in
construction, if not in language, is much superior
to the average ballad ; and the most obvious,
indeed the only feasible, explanation of this is that
it is merely a debased form of the Dalrymple
version, gradually debased since the ballad appeared
in Percy's *Reliques*.   But however that may be,
the masterly wording of the Dalrymple version,
the admirable art of its construction, the condensed,
dramatic force of the whole, and the wonderful

phrasing of the final stanza with the sudden revelation of the terrible climax, render it one of the most
outstanding specimens of existing British verse in
the old ballad form, but of verse with which the
desecrating muse of popular tradition has had, so
far as can be discerned, no commerce. Its final
stanza is an example, in its own fashion, of quite
perfect art :—

> " And what wull ye leive to your ain mither deir ?
>   My deir son now tell me O.
>   The curse of hell frae me sall ye beir,
>   Mither, mither :
>   The curse of hell frae me sall ye beir :
>   Sic counsells ye gave to me O."

And this fine dramatic close is thus naïvely
burlesqued in Motherwell's traditional version :—

> " What wilt thou leave to thy mother dear,
>   Son Davie, son Davie ?
>   A fire o' coals to burn her, wi' hearty cheer,
>   And she'll never get mair o' me."

Another excellent production is *Young Waters*
(94), published by Robert and Andrew Foulis,
1755. Its tragic art is not so perfect as that of
Edward, and it has some weak stanzas ; but it
introduces incremental repetition in a very effective
way to emphasise the sad plight of the doomed
youth :—

> " Aft I have ridden thro' Stirling town
>   In the wind bot and the weit ;
> Bot I neir rade thro' Stirling town
>   Wi fetters at my feit.
>
> Aft I have ridden thro' Stirling town
>   In the wind bot and the rain :
> But I neir rade thro' Stirling town
>   Neir to return again."

Inevitably a traditional copy of this ballad was discovered by Buchan ; but what he discovered was merely a bastard sample of the Foulis ballad, long previously published.

Then there is *Barbara Allan* (84), of which we first learn as " a little Scotch Song," with the singing of which Mrs Knipp the actress charmed the sentimental Pepys, and of which the best version is that printed in Ramsay's *Tea Table Miscellany*, the English version being merely a choice sample of stylish black-letter art :—

> " So this maid, she then did dye,
>   And desired to be buried by him ;
> And repented herself before she dy'd
>   That ever she did deny him."

Sir Patrick Spens (58), *Edom o' Gordon* (178), *The Bonnie Earl of Murray* (181), and other late Scottish ballads are referred to in the last chapter. *Johnie Cock* (114), a kind of Border ballad, but quite unhistorical, was evidently at one time a very effective dramatic piece. Several of the Robin Hood ballads are masterpieces of story-telling. A skilled art of narration, of dramatic presentation of incidents, is also conspicuous in many ballads which, for the most part, are now woeful examples both of rhyme and expression; and here and there we meet with isolated stanzas, matchless in their felicitous simplicity and their conveyance of tragic pathos. Are these examples of literary excellence, surviving amongst the imperfect traditional records, merely accidental or exceptional, or do they point to the previous existence of many ballads of real literary merit, ballads of interest not merely as vehicles of old legends or records of curious superstitions, but as examples of an ancient poetic art, not essentially faulty in rhyme and jejune in expression, but practised by men of some accomplishment, and now and again by men of genius ?

CHAPTER II

BALLAD THEMES

THE smallness of the proportion of ancient verse that has escaped oblivion, renders the great blank in British ballad literature less unaccountable than it might otherwise have been. Though, also, the old ballads and the ancient lyric verse are in this respect in rather a worse case than other forms of literature, the fact not only that they were meant to be sung, but that they were associated with forms of amusement frowned upon by the Church, largely explains this. The great prevalence of Puritanism, if only for a comparatively short time, in England, and its wider and longer prevalence in Scotland, also tended to the decay of interest in balladry in Britain.

For many centuries after the spread of Christianity throughout Europe, a large proportion of those nominally Christian were at heart pagan, and the earlier popular verse represented largely the pagan side of mediævalism. Even when they make mention of biblical characters, ballads are not weighted with Christian or religious purpose. They are largely destitute of moral aim ; the moral tag appended to some versions is a clear symptom of corruption. The story of what happened—its strangeness, its wonder, its awesomeness, its tragic horror, sometimes, though rarely, its great felicity—suffices.

As regards the themes of the ballad, their character and source is admirably indicated by Gaston Paris in the *Journal des Savants* for July 1898. " Ballads," he says, " are the work of poets of the later period of the Middle Ages "—that is, they are properly so, though ballads of a kind had also a later vogue—" and they have found their themes, to which they have given a colour strongly original, in popular tradition, in previous poems, in the romances of chivalry, in real events, and often in the imaginations of their authors, nourished by beliefs, superstitions, and reminiscences of all kinds current in a society where civilisation is scarcely yet established, and numerous vestiges still subsist of the barbarism and paganism that preceded Christianity."

Love is the theme of the larger number of the non-historical, and of several that are more or less historical. After the fashion of the older lyric verse, it is viewed as unamenable to restraint, but there is no brazen or alluring presentation of it as in some of the older lyric verse ; and it is oftener its tragic than its joyous aspect that is set forth.   What

the ballad chiefly exemplifies is the strength, the
supremacy, the fatefulness of the passion—a passion
against the gratification of which rank is no barrier,
which makes light of the opposition of relatives, is
blind to evil possibilities, and more frequently
brings woe than weal. But the tales of love which
they essay to set forth are evidently old tales, tales
of byegone generations, tales which derive their
credibility and much of their interest from the fact
that they represent a condition of society that is
strange to the experience of the listener.

A few of the old Scots or English ballads treat
of tragedies of elopement, or the perils and difficulties
of bride stealing—themes impressively dealt with
in some Danish ballads. In the later British ballads,
more or less founded on almost contemporary fact,
bride stealing usually ends in a rescue, but elope-
ments usually end successfully and to the special
advantage of the lovers. In the earlier love tragedies
an important part is played by the hostile brethren
—usually seven in number. Their opposition may
be due to different causes, and the form of the
ensuing tragedy also varies considerably. The
seven brethren figure with special effect in several
Scandinavian ballads ; and even in the mixed and
distorted English and Scottish brethren-tales there
are more than traces of dramatic impressiveness.
Earl Brand (7) has a close relation with the Danish

Ribold og Guldborg, and is probably a late derivation from it.

Sometimes the love tragedy is brought about by non-human personalities, as in the case of Mrs Jane Reynolds—of the seventeenth-century broadside, *James Harris* (243), doubtless founded on an older ballad—who, after her husband's absence at sea for seven years, married a carpenter, and was, later, lured away by a wicked spirit who appeared in the guise of her dead husband :—

> " And so together away they went
> From off the English shore."

But where they went, or how it came to be known that she eloped with a wicked spirit and not with her first husband, is not explained. In a Danish ballad a sprite assumes the guise of the lady's lover and carries her off; several Scandinavian ballads, probably of German origin, detail the tragic consequences of a maid having children by a Merman, or Hillman, or Dwarf King. In the very corrupt *Hynde Etin* (41), the tragic consequences are very much obscured ; but in one Scandinavian version, the lady, having revealed her connection with the dwarf, is compelled by him to return to the hill and dies the same night ; in other cases, after being permitted to revisit the earth, she refuses to return to her children, and is struck dead ; and in one instance she returns to her children and all is well. *Clerk Colvin* (42) details, in a fragmentary fashion, the fatal consequences of seeking a mermaid for a human bride, which is the subject of some striking Scandinavian versions derived from a Breton romance. The *Wee Wee Man* (38), of the Scottish ballad, displays no purpose except to impress one, who casually met him, with his superhuman strength and afford him a glimpse of the wonders of fairyland.

Several ballads detail the wiles of the Fairy Queen to get hold of a human lover. In a Danish ballad, of which there are also Norwegian and Swedish versions, she effects her purpose by giving the knight an elphin draught; but in *Thomas Rhymer* (37), derived from the old romance *Ogier le Danois*, her charms are a sufficient enticement. In the more complicated *Tamlane* (39), the lover was caught away by the Queen of the Fairies, while in a swoon, by falling from his horse, and while still under fairy detention is able to beguile a lady, who, from love of him or to save her babe from reproach, effects his release from fairyland by fearlessly following certain weird instructions of his in regard to disenchantment. A wonderfully good version of this ballad is preserved in the Glenriddel MS.; an excellent fragment, entitled " Kertonha," was collected by Herd; and with the aid of probably only these two versions, Burns constructed a version

C

for Johnson's *Museum*, which, here and there, bears
clear marks of his peculiar handiwork, as, for example,
in the following stanzas :—

> " Gloomy, gloomy, was the night,
>   And eerie was the way,
> As fair Jennie in her green mantle
>   To Mile's Cross she did gae.

> About the middle of the night
>   She heard the bridles ring ;
> The lady was as glad at that
>   As any earthly thing."

In some ballads the girl is enabled to save herself
from the wiles of a false lover by the aid of a witch,
or various magical devices.   Occasionally she does
so by superiority in a riddle game ; but, as a rule,
riddles are a kind of preliminary coquetry between
the lover and the maid, the lover winning her
consent by successful guessing of the riddle, as in
the case of *Captain Wedderburn* (46), which, however,
though included in Child's collection for the sake
of the riddle, is in no sense a traditional ballad, but
evidently an eighteenth century production of,
probably, some Edinburgh bard.

Jealousy and rivalry supply varied material for
poignant ballad tragedies. *The Twa Sisters*, or
The Cruel Sister (10), of which the traditional
Scottish versions are related to a broadside of 1656

or its derivatives, is notable for introducing a very old harp or viol tale, connected with a group of stories prevalent throughout the old world of Europe, Asia and Africa : a portion of the drowned lady's body—her hair or her veins for the strings of a viol or harp, and her fingers for the pegs of a viol—having been used for part of a musical instrument, it makes known her death at the hands of her sister. Evidently the broadside is derived from a translation of one of the Danish versions. This form of the story is also comparatively modern, a misreading of the old superstition of the soul embodying itself in a tree above the grave, the viol being made of its wood.

The rivalry of two brothers is the theme of a very tragic Danish ballad, *Angelfyr og Kelmer Kamp,* founded on an old saga—the one brother killing the other in a duel and the survivor being felled dead by his father. In another, *Ebbe Skammelson,* one brother having circulated the story that the other is dead, marries his betrothed bride, and the tricked lover kills both the brother and the bride.

In *Young Hunting* (68) and *Earl Richard* (68)— of the Herd MS.—the lady, quite after the modern fashion, murders her false lover ; and the murder is revealed by a bird, which, according to an old superstition not here preserved, must have been the slain lover, who assumed this form to denounce the murder. *Young Hunting* is a very ragged production, having suffered severely at the rough hands of the traditional muse, as witness :—

> " She has birld in him, young Hunting,
>   The good ale and the wine,
>   Till he was as fou drunken
>   As any wild-wood swine."

But it includes in it two other interesting superstitions, that of the candle burning more brightly above the pool containing a drowned person, and that of the ordeal by fire. The fragmentary *Earl Richard* is both better rhymed and more refined in its phraseology. It evidently formed part of a comparatively undebased production, *e.g.*

> " They have booted him and spurred him,
>   As he was wont to ride :
>   A hunting-horn around his waist,
>   A sharp sword by his side."

In *Young Benjie* (86), which may be a variant of *Young Hunting*, and in which the jealous lover throws the lady over the linn, it is the corpse itself that, " at the dead hour of the night," reveals the murder.

In *Lord Randal* (12), more a popular rhyme than a ballad and probably transferred to Scotland from Italy, we have an instance of a lover being poisoned by his sweetheart, but for what reason is not revealed.

The method of telling the story is artful, though in most versions it is spoiled by too great diffuseness. In striking contrast with them is the version sent by Burns to Johnson's *Museum*, where the narration is confined to two stanzas with consummate artistic effect.

The various English and Scottish ballads—*Lord Thomas and Fair Annet* (73), *Lord Thomas and Fair Elinor* (73), *Fair Margaret and Sweet William* (74), and *Fair Margaret's Misfortune* (74)—in which the nut-brown maid or the brown lady, which Lord Thomas or Sweet William had married for her money, causes the death of the true love, are merely different versions of the same story, and there are, also, a number of Scandinavian versions. The traditional Scottish versions are evidently derived from the broadside copies. The *Lord Thomas and Fair Annet* version, transmitted to Percy from Scotland, is much superior to the others ; but the vernacular is too rude and awkward to be quite consistent with what may be termed the excellence of the narrative as drama. This version could certainly not have become what it was by mere tradition, and was probably revised, not merely by Percy, but by the transmitter. However that may be, the mingled—good and bad—character of its vernacular so detracts from its effect, as to make it difficult for probably most Scots to agree with the, otherwise, partly justifiable verdict of Professor Child, that "it is one of the most beautiful of all ballads." Nor are the two following stanzas master-pieces of incremental repetition :—

> " My maids, gae to my dressing-room
> And dress to me my hair :
> Where eir ye laid a plait before,
> See ye lay ten times mair.
>
> My maids, gae to my dressing-room
> And dress to me my smock ;
> The one half is o' the holland fine,
> The other o' needle-work."

In the *Lord Thomas and Fair Annet* story, Lord Thomas kills the wicked nut-brown maid and then commits suicide ; in the more tender *Sweet William* tale, the sight of William and his bride riding to the church causes the lady to die of " pure true love." Her ghost appears at William's bedfoot on the wedding night, and makes him dream a dream so ominous of evil that he rides next day to Fair Margaret's bower, and, after beholding the corpse of his dead mistress, dies of sorrow. In both ballads occurs the story of the intertwining shrubs, derived from the superstition already mentioned (p. 35). In an allied ballad, *Lord Lovel* (75), the lady dies owing to the long unexplained absence of her lover, and the lover dies of grief and remorse, an easily conceived tragedy, if it but seldom happens. The *Fair Annie* ballad (62), which appears in Scott's *Minstrelsy* as *Lord Thomas* and *Fair Annie*, and in Jamieson's *Ballads* as *Burd Ellen*, is another ballad on a similar theme. Here the bride, on learning that the husband's mistress, who had seven sons by him, was her sister, returns home. In its plot the story closely resembles the Scandinavian *Skiœn Anna*, but it is very imperfectly told in the British versions. The Danish ballad evidently derives from a German one. The story, which is the theme of the Breton Romance, *Le Lai del Freisne*, or *The Lay of the Ash*, is found in various modified forms in other Danish, and in German, Spanish and Swedish ballads ; but its wide-spread character need not imply a common origin, for the plot is really very simple.

Various poignantly dramatic situations are developed with some skill from forced marriages, especially when the lady is found to be with child to the true love, as, for example, in the case of *Fair Janet* (64), who, after giving birth secretly to a child, is, next day, married, pale and wan, to an old lord, and in dancing after the marriage feast with her lover falls dead at his feet. Other forms of the illicit love tragedy occur from the lady admitting the wrong person to her chamber, as the harper's page instead of the harper in *Glasgerion* (67); the page and lady receiving their death at the hands of the harper, after which he loses his reason. In the case of *Clerk Saunders* (69), the lover is killed while asleep by the seven brothers, and the lady knows nothing, until on the morrow she awakes with the dead blood-stained corpse beside her. Again, in a Danish ballad, *Habor og Signold*, Habor, the royal Prince, gains access to the royal princess, Signold, disguised as a lady, but is betrayed by her maid ; and on witnessing her lover being brought out to be hanged, she sets fire to her bower and perishes in the flames.

The woes of a lady who finds herself *enceinte* and whose lover will not, at first, agree to marry her, but is overcome on hearing her moaning after childbirth and the cries of his infant son, is the subject of the artless and affecting *Child Waters* (63). All here ends happily, but not so in a French ballad, *L'accouchment au Bois*, which M. Gaston Paris supposes to be the original—the theme being oriental—of the Danish *Redselille og Medelvold* and various German versions. The two lovers take to flight, and the lady, having swooned in a wood, the lover hastens to fetch water for her, and, after dis-covering it with some difficulty, finds his mistress lying dead and two dead infants beside her. He buries them and then commits suicide. A some-what similar tale is told in *The Cruel Mother* (20), the original source of the traditional versions being pro-bably a black-letter broadside, *The Duke's Daughter's*

Cruelty (*c.* 1683), which very closely resembles a
Danish version and most likely has a modern connection with it. In this instance the lady kills the
children, and after being accosted and reproached
by their ghosts, dies " away in sad despair."

In the *Lass of Lochroyall* or *Roch Royall* (76)—
which, in the versions that survive, is a rhetorical
and high sounding, but evidently very corrupt, production—the lady gives birth to a son in her lover's
absence and sails over " the salt sea " to seek him
in a mysterious castle, where he is either detained
by enchantment or denied to her by the falsehoods
of his mother. According to one version they are
drowned in the sight of the distracted lover ; according to another he sees the corpse as it is being
carried to burial ; and in all versions he dies of a
broken heart and, as usual, they are buried together.

Detention, by an evil personage or spirit or by
enchantment, is a common ballad theme. Scandinavian ballads record how a knight by means of
runes wins a bride in a cave in which she is detained
by a witch ; and a Shetland ballad, *King Orfeo* (19),
of Danish origin, tells how a king by his skill on the
pipes induced the King of the Fairies to give him
back his wife. Most commonly the enchantment
consists in transformation into a bird or hind or
some monster form. The story of a girl changed
periodically into a hind and killed in the chase, is the

theme of a popular French ballad, *La Blanche biche*. Restoration is difficult and requires the observance of some kind of rite, either disagreeable or fenced by terrors. In *Tamlane* the enchanted person is made to assume terrible shapes to frighten her deliverer from doing what is necessary ; and in a Danish ballad we have the case of a lady whom, as a nightingale, her brother brought home and placed in a cage, when she assumed the form of different wild beasts until he cut her with his penknife, when she at once stood before him as his sister. In other instances the monster, as in *Kemp Owyne* (34), must be kissed. *The Marriage of Sir Gawain* (31), again, represents a common tale of an unseemly lady being changed into a fair maid after being bedded with a knight ; and a similar instance is recorded in *King Henry* (32), probably a modern adaptation of a Gaelic tale : a princess, who had been bewitched into a ghastly shape by her stepdame's skill, being disenchanted by the king's son having intercourse with her. In the Danish *Valravnen*, a lady's brother, who had been transformed into a raven, is restored after pecking out the right eye of her child and drinking some of its blood ; in the case of a Werwolf maiden, restoration is effected by the monster biting her little brother and sucking the blood ; and a maiden transformed into a hawk is restored by her lover giving her flesh from his own breast. These different instances seem to point to the infusion into the bewitched person of some human influence, as an essential to deliverance from the physical thraldom.

Tragedies originating in the revenge of adultery are a common theme. One of the most painful is that in *Child Maurice* (83). A lady having asked her illegitimate son to meet her in Silverwood, her husband, under the delusion that he is her lover, kills him and scornfully presents her with his head, which she recognises as that of her son. Under the title *Gil Morice*, a version of the ballad was printed by Foulis in 1755, evidently retouched and somewhat modernised, but with all its faults and imperfect emendations, a very pungent production. It suggested to Home his tragedy of *Douglas*, and Gray wrote of it to Mason : " It is divine." The version in the Percy MS. lacks much of its graphic force. In *Little Musgrave* (81), the husband, after slaying the lover and the lady, immediately repents, for ballads represent the deeds and sentiments of persons that are governed mainly by the primitive emotions. In a similar case, *Old Robin of Portingale* (80), the avenger also repents ; but, here, the age of the husband may be supposed to account both for the unfaithfulness of the wife and his own maudlin change of mood, though his age is, of course, quite inconsistent with his exceptional prowess in slaying the four and twenty knights. The wildness of the ballad's melodrama is, in fact, a certain sign of great corruption, though the only version preserved, that in the Percy MS., is in parts vivid and picturesque. *Jellon Grame* (90), of which all the copies are very modern in style, records how a lover in order to escape the vengeance of his sweetheart's father, should it be known that she had given birth to a child, murders her immediately after the birth and buries her in a wood, but saves the child, who, having, when he came to manhood, been told by his father of the tragedy, shoots him through with an arrow at the grave of his mother. In *Sir Aldingar* (59), of which the earliest version is a rather halting one in the Percy MS., we have a theme which is the subject of ballads, tales and romances in Scandinavia, Germany, France, Italy, and Spain, and apparently has some foundation in fact. In the English version a false steward, to take revenge on the Queen, because, in the King's absence she had refused his advances, puts a blind and lame lazar man in her bed just before the King returns, and shows him there to the King. The lady affirms that she is betrayed by the steward, and declares that had she been a man she would have put the case to the trial of combat. The King thereupon gives her forty days in which to find a champion, and at last one is found, in the English version a dwarf, apparently non-human. He slays the false steward, who, before dying, confesses his guilt, and the lazar man becomes steward in his stead.

A very imperfect and confused ballad records how the *Clerks twa sons of Owsenford* (72) while at the university—possibly at Oxford, for there may be some confusion in the title—were hanged by the mayor for seducing his two daughters; but, though a similar theme is the subject of various foreign ballads, it is but seldom that the law interferes with love episodes

Various Yarrow ballads (214, 215) record the treacherous death of a husband, or lover, of lower rank than the wife, or sweetheart. In some versions the lover is slain by armed men—an echo perhaps of the seven hostile brethren—on the braes of Yarrow : in others he is found drowned in that euphonious river ; and mangled versions of the story—doubtless of broadside or chap-book origin— are associated with the water of Gamrie and the river Clyde. The oldest printed version of a Yarrow ballad is the black-letter (*c.* 1690) *Delectable New Ballad, intituled Leader-Haughs and Yarrow,* ostensibly by Nicol Burn, the violer. It is merely a descriptive eulogy of the district ; but all the tragic ballads are in the same measure. The oldest of them, *Willie's Rare and Willie's Fair,* which first appeared in Thomson's *Orpheus,* 1733, merely tells the story of a lover amissing on the eve of his marriage, and at last found drowned :—

> " She sought him east, she sought him west,
>   She sought him brade and narrow,
>   Syne in the clifting of a craig
>   She found him drowned in Yarrow."

And it is by no means impossible that the detailed tragic versions are merely later inventions suggested by the song. In any case they seem to borrow their circumstantiality from the tale told in *The Duke of Athole's Nurse* (212)—of which all the versions are very imperfectly rhymed and fragmentary—the story being that of a lover betrayed by his leman to her brothers, in some instances the traditional seven, while in an ale-house. This ballad may, however, be merely a mangled version of the more detailed and coherent *Sir James the Rose* (213).

A few ballads deal with the tragedy of love between brother and sister. In most cases they are ignorant of the kinship and are the mere victims of blind chance, a fact which causes commiseration to predominate over horror. Akin to them is the Danish story, possibly founded on fact, of the three robbers—in early youth stolen from home by a robber band and trained by them to the profession —who, meeting three ladies in a wood, give them the choice of death or marriage, and on their refusal

of marriage, slay them one by one, shortly after
which the father discovers that they are his sons
and that they had slain their sisters.   The same
story is also substantially told in the Scottish ballad
Babylon, or *The Bonnie Banks of Fordie* (14), in
two line stanzas like the Danish one and evidently
derived from it.   In another Danish ballad, brother
and sister fall in love, but the kinship is made known
by the mother when told of their intention to wed.
In *The Bonnie Hynd* (50), much modernised and,
it may be, a traditional version from a broadside,
the lady, on learning the relationship, commits
suicide.   *The King's Dochter, Lady Jean* (52), is a
very silly, corrupt and vulgar derangement of the
same story.   The lady, having sorely wounded herself by the commonplace penknife, returns home in
great weakness, explaining that a heavy stone had
fallen upon her breast from a castle wa'.   Then—

> " Her brither he came trippin doun the stair,
>   His steps they were fu' slow ;
> He sank into his sister's arms
>   And they died as white as snow."

A quite choice sample of the excruciating bathos
of the popular muse.   But *Sheath and Knife* (16)—or
The Broom blooms bonnie—which relates a similar
story, manifests traces of dramatic pathos and
accomplished art.   The lady gives directions to her

brother-lover how to kill her, and tells him she will
give him the signal by " a loud cry " :—

> " Now when he heard her gie a loud cry,
>   His silver arrow from his bow he suddenly let fly :
>   Now they'll never gang doun to the brome onie mair.

> " He has made a grave that was lang and was deep,
>   And he has buried his sister, wi' her babe at her feet ;
>   And they'll never gang doun to the brume onie mair."

In *Lizie Wan* (51), a debased version of this or a
similar ballad, and much modernised, there is no
ignorance of relationship in the case either of brother
or sister ; and the brother, on learning that she has
told her parents their secret, cuts off her head and
mangles her in savage fashion. Then, after an
interview with his mother, he declares his intention
to escape his father's wrath by setting out to sea,
and allowing the boat to sink with him :—

> " And when will thou come hame again
>   O my son Geordie Wan ?
>   The sun and the moon shall dance on the green
>   That night when I come hame."

In various ballads the plot turns on an absent
lover or husband and the final reunion. A notable
instance is *Young Beichan* (53), or *Lord Bateman*.
While affected by the legend of Gilbert Becket, it
enshrines a story common throughout Europe,

originally coloured with incidents peculiar to the Middle Ages and the subject of various romances and numerous ballads. *Young Beichan* is, however, very much modernised in its setting as well as in its tone, all the magic and necromancy of the older narration being omitted, and the whole evidently a mere debased travesty of an original now lost. In *Hind Horn* (17) the plot is evolved by the aid of a magic ring. It is in two line stanzas, and tells substantially the story of Henry of Brunswick, which is the theme of an old German romance and of a Danish and German ballad. Other Danish ballads more closely follow the story of the Horn romances than does the English ballad.

Neither magic nor adventure in far countries has a place in *The Broom of Cowdenknows* (217), which has an entirely rustic setting : the knight, who had taken advantage of a girl " milking her father's ewes," comes riding past the farm some years afterwards with a troop of merry gentlemen, and seeing her with the child, marries her and makes her a lady. Possibly the ballad may be related to the old *Brume, brume on hill*, mentioned in *The Complaynt of Scotland* ; but most versions make no mention either of the " brume " or of Cowdenknows. The black-letter, *Northern Lass* (of 1629), " set to a pleasant Scotch tune, called " The Broom of Cowdenknowes," is a quite different

D

ballad.   Evidently it was the black-letter that
suggested the *Cowdenknows* ballad of Ramsay's *Tea
Table Miscellany*.   An innocent ballad—a modern
adaptation of an old theme—tells how *The Bailiff's
Daughter of Islington* (105) travelled the by no
means long distance from Islington to London to
find her true-love, whom she had thought to "have
seen no more."

Wanton, unexplained, or excessive crime is set
forth, in its naked abnormality, in different ballads,
with varying degrees of effectiveness.   In *Young
Johnstone* (88), of which there is a spirited fragment
in the Herd MS., the false knight, after killing the
brother of his mistress, is sheltered from the avengers
in her secret bower, and as she, later, enters it he
draws his sword and stabs her dead, but whether
from suspicion of betrayal, or by mistake, or im-
pelled by mere mad, murderous wickedness, is not
made clear.   In *Edward* (13), the wife, by some
kind of evil suggestion, causes her son to murder
his father; but no reason is given except deadly
and wicked hatred on her part, hatred which causes
the son to evoke on her " the curse of hell."   The
wild revenge of a mason, because the owner of a
castle which he built finds it impossible to grant
him immediate payment, is depicted with some art
in a savage ballad, *Lammikin* (93).   Even in several
of the untouched versions that survive — all the

versions are in the exceptional seven six metre—
the tragedy is set forth with curious dramatic
vividness, though most are spoiled with diffuse
repetition. With the connivance of a false nurse,
the mason kills the babe, and the lady, lured down
by its cry, is also slain. *Queen Eleanor's Confession*
(156), even as it appears in a halting broadside of
1685, is a keenly caustic production, and if, as
Professor Child affirmed, in the " truly popular tone,"
must have become so by popular deterioration, though
the broadside is not so deteriorated as the traditional
versions of which it is the source.

The common superstition of the return of the
dead was bound to attract the attention of balladists
Sometimes the ghost of a murdered person returns
to make known the crime ; but the return of the
dead drawn by the power of love, a belief probably
suggested by the experience of dreams, is a much
more moving theme. The *Suffolk Miracle* (272),
a broadside of 1689, records, in a prosy, wooden
fashion, how a dead man in the middle of the night
carries off his mistress, ignorant of his death, on
horseback from the place where she was staying,
brings her to her parents' house and then disappears.
A modified form of the same story, more detailed
and much more picturesque, is the subject of a
West of England tale ; and it forms the theme of a
Breton romance, *Le Frère de Lait*, and of Bürger's

Leonora, suggested by the German ballad *Lenore*.
A very popular, but rather gruesome, Danish ballad
tells of a dead knight who visited his mistress with
his coffin on his back. She walked beside him to
the churchyard, when he suddenly disappeared into
the earth ; and within a month she died and was,
of course, buried beside him. This ballad bears
some similarity to *Sweet William's Ghost* (77),
published in Ramsay's *Tea Table Miscellany* , and
probably not exactly as he got it. The version of
the ballad in the Herd MS. appears to be a kind of
sequel to *Clerk Saunders* (69) : a victim of the seven
hostile brethren visits his mistress from the grave,
to ask again for " her faith and troth." She gives
it him, upon which he affirms that if " ever the dead
comes for the quick " he will come again for her.
Apparently she expected to die in giving birth to
a child, for she asks him what becomes of women
who die " in strong travelling," and he tells her :—

> " Their beds are made in the Heavens high,
> ⸕Down at the foot of our gud Lord's knee,
> Well set about wi' gilly-flowers,
> A wat sweet company for to see."

Fragmentary, imperfectly expressed and rhymed,
and more than a little incoherent though it be, it,
even in its ruined condition, preserves traces of an
original ballad of more than average merit. *Proud*

Lady Margaret (47), first published in Scott's
"Minstrelsy," and of which there are Laing and
Buchan perversions, is, itself, probably a mangled and
perverted version of *Sweet William's Ghost*. Hamilton,
an Edinburgh music-seller, and the author of some
Scottish songs, who stated he obtained it from his
mother's recitation, afterwards sent to Scott a
riddle addition, which simply heightened the ballad's
incongruity.

The very fragmentary *Wife of Usher's Well* (79),
first published in Scott's "Minstrelsy," from the recitation of a West Lothian dame, tells of the return at
night of an old woman's three sons who had been
drowned at sea. It is interesting as preserving an
old superstition of the sacredness of the birch.
Versions in Peeblesshire, Shropshire and America
indicate the probable existence of a broadside
version. Evidently the Scott version has been
here and there amended, for it rhymes admirably ;
but the last stanza is symptomatic of the rustic
muse of West Lothian :—

> " Fare ye well, my Mother dear !
> Farewell to barn and byre !
> And fare ye well, the bonny lass
> That kindles my mother's fire."

A Scandinavian ballad tells the story of a dead
mother's return to the earth to visit her children,

oppressed by a wicked step-mother, and induce her
husband to take their part and care for them ; a
theme which is widely spread and probably came
to Scandinavia from France.

The early British ballads of adventure are confined mainly to the Robin Hood series. The historical ballads do not relate events earlier than
the fourteenth century—with the partial exception
of *The Gude Wallace* (157), which is a late derivative
from Blind Harry's poem. Perhaps the oldest of
the historical ballads is that recording *Hugh Spencer's
Feats in France* (158), of which a version is preserved
in the Percy MS. A ballad on *Durham Field* (159),
17th October 1346, avowedly tells of what happened
long previously :—

> " For as it befell in Edward the Third's days,
>   In England where he ware the crown."

And neither *The Battle of Otterbourne* (161) nor
The Hunting of the Cheviot (162) professes to record
events that are contemporaneous, whatever earlier
ballads may have done :—

> " Yt fell abowght the Lamasse tyde,
>   Whan husbond wynnes ther haye."

And again :—

> " A woeful hunting once there did
>   in Chevy Chase befall."

In France, Italy, Provence and Spain—one or two doubtful cases excepted—no events earlier than the sixteenth century are commemorated in ballads ; but Scandinavia, besides ballads of adventure derived from the old sagas, possesses others dealing with historical events of the thirteenth century.

Many ballad themes are common to all the countries of Europe—some for the simple reason that human nature and events possessed throughout these countries a fundamental similarity, others because of the wide-spread character of certain legends and superstitions, and a third class owing to their derivation from the same or similar old romances. But even when there is considerable similarity in theme, there is usually a great diversity in details and in the method of treatment, a diversity indicating a difference in authorship and original construction. In the case, however, of certain Danish and British ballads, there is apparent indication that the theme reached the one country from the óther in the form of a ballad, as there is also evidence of a similar transmission between the different countries of Scandinavia. So far, however, as surviving evidence enables us to determine, the connection between Denmark and this country as regards even ballad themes is comparatively slight ; the difference in the themes and in the treatment of them are overwhelmingly more numerous and greater than the identities or similarities ; and Scandinavia, while possessing many ballad themes of native derivation, has, as regards its non-native themes, a closer connection with France and the Latin countries than with Britain.   Here there is evidence of her dependence ; but it is a matter of doubt whether she is at all dependent on Britain (if she is it is on Danish Britain), or Britain—apart from exceptional cases—is dependent on her.   And again, if Britain is dependent on her, there is the question whether that dependence is early or late.

CHAPTER III

THE ORIGIN AND AUTHORSHIP OF BALLADS

How did the traditional ballad, as we now know it, originate ? When did it come into vogue ? These are questions in regard to which there is comparatively little direct evidence ; and if there is much circumstantial evidence, it is rather complex and intricate, and there is by no means perfect agreement as to its interpretation. A preliminary difficulty is that nearly all the ballad versions that survive in MS. are of comparatively late date ; and that, with few exceptions, all the early ballads have been greatly modified by tradition—so much so, that it is by no means easy to tell what was the original character of the literary expression of many. Some even hold that they never had what may be termed literary characteristics, that they are essentially traditional, that, like Topsy, they were not made, but grew, and that certain of them have practically existed in traditional form from immemorial ages.

The main ground for this assumption is, that some of them embody legends and superstitions of very ancient origin and of very widespread diffusion.

If, for example, a British ballad embodies a legend common throughout Europe, it is inferred that during generations of unknown number it has been transmitted in verse form of some kind from nation to nation and from one language to another, until by the processes of tradition it has gradually assumed its present shape ; or as Professor Child—who, however, did not share the opinion—put it, it is supposed that to explain its existence, we have to go " back almost to the cradle of mankind, to a primeval common ancestry of all or most of the nations amongst whom it appears."

A somewhat similar if vaguer theory—partly suggested by the character of certain ballad themes, partly by the literary characteristics of the ballad, or its lack of literary characteristics, as manifested in the traditional versions—is that the ballad (to use the words of Signor A. Bartoli, in reference to the views of certain persons regarding popular poetry generally, as quoted in M. Alfred Jeanroy's *Poésie Lyrique en France*, p. xi.) is the spontaneous creation of certain epochs, " favourable, as they put it, in terms more pompous than precise, to the production of a non self-conscious and impersonal poetry, springing from the heart of the people." Some have even gone beyond this : to confound the ballad with the most ancient form of the tale, by describing it in general terms as a product of the "popular imagination," and the creation of the "folk fancy." Such conceptions M. Jeanroy, again, regards as more or less "mystic and superstitious." They have, he says, "the double drawback of deceiving by a phrase and frustrating serious research ; in effect, it seems that when one has said of any particular specimen of verse that it has its source in popular poetry, we have said the last word on the subject, and there is nothing more to be done but reverently to bow down before the mysterious agency of nature." "In this sense," he also goes on to say, "it would evidently be very incorrect to describe our ancient lyric verse as popular poetry. If, on the contrary, by this phrase is meant simply productions emanating, without doubt, from individual poets possessed of a certain culture and producing work reflective and literary, but yet in such rapport with the people as to utter its thought and sentiment and appeal to its heart—pieces, in short, composed not by the people, but for the people and for all the people—we believe that the convenient term is sufficiently exact and that it might be preserved."

In an article on the ballad in Johnson's *Encyclopedia*—which, however, he did not desire to be "regarded as final"—Professor Child expressed a somewhat similar yet, in some respects, different opinion, with addenda which tend to emphasize the difference. He describes " the historical and natural place " of the ballad as " anterior to the appearance of the poetry of art, to which it has formed a step, and by which it has been regularly displaced, and in some cases all but extinguished." " The condition of society," he also says, " in which a truly national or popular poetry appears, explains the character of such poetry. It is a condition in which the people are not divided by political organization and book culture into markedly distinct classes, in which, consequently, there is such community of ideas and feelings that the whole people form one individual. Such poetry, accordingly, while it is in its essence an expression of our common human nature, and so of universal and indestructible interest, will in each case be differentiated by circumstances and idiosyncracy. On the other hand, it will always be an expression of the mind and heart of the people as an individual and never of the personality of individual men. The fundamental characteristic of popular ballads is, therefore, the absence of subjectivity and of self-consciousness. Though they do not write themselves, as William Grimm has said, though a man and not a people has composed them, still the author counts for nothing, and it is not by mere accident, but with the best reasons that they have come down to us anonymous." Further, he expresses the opinion that " the incidents of many ballads are such as might occur anywhere, and at any time, and with regard to agreements that cannot be expressed in this way, we have only to remember that tales and songs were the chief social amusement of all classes of people in all the nations of Europe during the Middle Ages, and that new stories would be eagerly sought for by those whose business it was to furnish this amusement, and be rapidly spread among the fraternity. A great effect was undoubtedly produced by the crusades, which both brought the chief European nations into closer intercourse and made them acquainted with the East."

Combining the statements of Child in his Cyclopedia article with various dicta in the prefaces to different ballads, Mr W. M. Hart, in the *Publications of the Modern Language Association of America for* 1906, after recording them, thus sums up Child's " conception of the popular ballad." " He regarded it as a distinct species of poetry which precedes the poetry of art, as the product of a homogeneous people, the expression of our common human nature, of the mind and heart of the people, never of the personality of an individual man, devoid, therefore, of all subjectivity and self-consciousness. Hence the author counts for nothing." Child's explanation of similarity in the plots of ballads of different nations and his assignment of the authorship of ballads to individuals are passed by. A summary cannot include everything, but these are important, even cardinal, omissions; for the statements of Child imply (1) that ballads generally, or at least the ballads known to us, are not earlier than the crusades; (2) that though popular, and usually drawing their material from popular sources, they are not of popular, in the sense of being of communal, origin, but have all an individual authorship; (3) that they were the work, many of them at least, of a fraternity whose " tales and songs were the chief social amusement of all classes of people." From the perusal merely of Mr Hart's summary, we could not even infer that Child definitely attributed individual authorship to the ballad. On the contrary, we would be apt to conclude that he deemed it the mysterious creation of the " popular imagination," the combined achievement of " a homogeneous people," which, by means of it, found expression for " its mind and heart."

But while Mr Hart seems, therefore, to have, unconsciously, rendered the views of Child a little more akin than Child intended to the " popular imagination " theory, the character of Child's statements may partly excuse this. We are told, for example, that " the author counts for nothing." He made the ballad—this Child affirms, though the summary of Mr Hart may leave it an open question—and yet he counts for nothing ! Why ? Apparently because the ballad is " an expression of our common human nature," of " the mind and heart of the people as an individual, and never of the personality of individual men." But what do these pronouncements exactly signify ? Do they mean merely that the ballad belongs to that class of verse, which, to use the words of M. Jeanroy, " instead of expressing the author's own sentiments, paints character, recounts an adventure, creates personages ; so that it is unnecessary that he should manifest himself in his work, except as actor or author of the scene he describes, it being enough that his work is objective ? " Child may have meant partly this, but he evidently meant something more. While, if he assumes, he does not distinctly state that the ballad is objective, he lays special stress on the fact that it is " an expression of the mind and heart of the people as an individual." In his view, the reason why the personality of the author does not manifest itself in the ballad, is because the sentiments it expresses are those of " our common human nature," and this for the reason that the ballad belongs to an age when there were no definite class distinctions, and therefore such " a community of ideas and feelings that the whole people form one individual." But to find such a society would it not be necessary to go almost to the cradle of mankind ? Whereas, have we not been told that ballads are the work of a special fraternity in the Middle Ages and intended for the amusement of all classes ? Nay, if Child's words be interpreted literally, how in a society with no idiosyncratic peculiarities would it be possible to find ballad themes, for do not ballads derive their special interest largely from the fact that they narrate exceptional deeds or events ? True, they appeal mainly to the common emotions of human nature, to the sense of wonder, pity, horror, awe ; but many other forms of verse appeal to man's common emotions. As already stated, ballads are not, as a rule, burdened with any moral lesson, they are destitute of didactic intent, they are not reflective in tone, or expressive of special individual moods, or a record of individual experience, or a manifestation of idiosyncrasies of thought or sentiment peculiar to the author. But various other forms of verse are in this sense impersonal. This was the tendency of nearly all the older verse; and most of the old surviving songs, and many of the new ones, are, in essence, " an expression of our common human nature " ; they appeal to every one without distinction of class. So do the greater dramas, the dramas of Greece and Shakespeare, if not of Shaw and Ibsen. Also, much of the higher emotional literature tends to do so ; for it emanates from the permanent realities, not from the passing fashions and conventions, of life. This is its title to exemption from earthly oblivion ; and even the ballad, as we know it, with all its traditional excrescences, defects and malformations, possesses, by virtue of the character of its aim and appeal, its peculiar method and its emotional sincerity, a certain permanent interest. The romance, from which it often borrowed its themes, has now become archaic : the life has gone out of it ; but the ballad has laid hold of its essence, and in a condensed form recreated it. Though often concerned with a past strangely different from our present, with semi-savage conditions of society, and superstitions wellnigh extinct, it yet often appeals with curious dramatic intensity to the primary passions and emotions. In this sense the ballad is certainly impersonal ; but while doubtless holding it to be impersonal in this sense, Child also clearly held it to be impersonal in another. He held it to be so in the sense that " the author counts for nothing," counts so absolutely for nothing that it is " with the best reasons " it " has come down to us anonymous." Of course, in addition to the ballad, much old verse " has come down to us anonymous " : some of the best of the old lyrics are so ; but it would seem that the ballad is anonymous by a special providence of its own, and a providence entirely in accordance with the fitness of things.

E

Why, then, are we to accept, not merely without regret, but with special satisfaction, this decree of providence about the ballad ?   How is it that here alone in literature the author " counts for nothing ? " The author of anything must count—if we may put it so—for everything, so far as that thing is concerned, though the merely mechanical maker of anything can hardly be termed the author of it : he is only an imitator, not a creator.   Therefore the mere fact that any form of literature is impersonal, does not justify the statement that the author of it counts for nothing.   *God save the King* is impersonal, so is *The Marseillaise,* and so are *Scots wha hae* and *Auld Lang Syne* : even though not epical or dramatic, though subjective rather than objective, they express common and not individual sentiments.   And yet does the author of them count for nothing ?

What, then, is the specific difference between them and the ballad that prompted Child's unique pronouncement about the ballad ?   It would appear to be not merely that the ballad is the expression of " our common human nature," but a common, undistinguished expression of it, an expression of it wholly lacking in individual art.   We are, in fact, told that the ballad is anterior to the poetry of art. But what, again, does this mean ?   Can there, in the strictest sense, be a poetry anterior to the poetry of art ? Is poetry not like painting or music, essentially an art ? Is the ballad wholly artless ? Is there no art in its metrical arrangement, in its rhyme, in its diction, in its construction as a complete whole, in its dramatic form, in its method of evolving the situation, in its use — in many ballads—of a peculiarly effective refrain. And was there no poetry of art anterior to the crusades ? Some hold, as we shall see, that this is largely, mainly or wholly, communal art ; but not so Child. While affirming that it is " with the best reasons " the ballad has come down to us anonymous, he yet attributes to it an individual authorship. What, then, are " the best reasons " for its providential anonymity ? They would appear to be mainly one : that so essentially popular is it in its theme and the character of its appeal, that it matters nothing who its original author may have been, or how it was originally composed. So completely common must it be (so it would seem), both in style and matter, that no curiosity need be felt as to who wrote it. The proper destiny of its author is inglorious obscurity, and its appropriate place is enshrinement in the heart and memory of the people.

But while such a theory seems to lack consistency and coherence, it also takes a great deal for granted. It implies that we have a pretty definite knowledge of the style, expression and construction of each ballad as it came from the brain of its author, whereas our knowledge of most ballads is a knowledge of them only as preserved in tradition, and often in the tradition of many generations. The reasoning of Child on this point seems, therefore, to move mainly in a vicious circle, for it is not only conceivable but actually certain, that many ballads owe much of the " impersonality " that now characterizes them, much of the similarity in phraseology and manner, many of their peculiar lapses in rhyme, much of what is described as " truly popular " in their style, much of their jejuneness and commonness, to the influence of their long enshrinement in the people's memory and their long contact with its mind and heart.

And the strange thing is that Child himself has practically said so. " At every stage of oral transmission," so has he incidentally remarked, " we must suppose that some accidental variations from what was delivered would be introduced and occasionally some wilful variations. Memory will fail at times ; at times the listener will hear amiss or will not understand, and a perversion of sense will ensue or absolute nonsense—nonsense which will be servilely repeated, and which repetition may make more gross." He affirms that in tradition, even in the best of it, the ballad " departs from the original form," and he has special praise for those of the Robin Hood ballads, which, having been early preserved in MS., " have come down to us in comparatively ancient form." Of *Robin Hood and the Monk* (119) he wrote : " Too much could not be said in praise of this ballad, but nothing need be said. It is very perfect of its kind ; and yet we have others equally good, and beyond doubt should have had more, if they had been written down early, as this was, and had not been left to the chances of tradition. Even writing would not have saved all, but writing has saved this (in large part), and in excellent form." But if this be so, what a different, how much more correct and evidently how much higher an estimate we might have formed of the achievements of the old balladists, had they, themselves, got their verses written down, so that they might possibly, many of them, have come down to us unimproved by amenders and unimpaired by tradition ! And had the authors' names been attached to them, surely so much the better, so much the more in accordance with the fitness of things ! And yet we are told of this fine ballad, with its consummate introductory stanzas, already quoted (p. 11) ; of *Sir Patrick Spens* (58), regarding which Child affirmed it would be hard to find in ballad poetry or elsewhere " happier or more refined touches " than those in two of its stanzas ; of *Edward* (13), the language of which is, we are told, apart from the word " brand,"

" entirely fit," entirely fit in the ballad sense ; of the *Lochmaben Harper* (192), pronounced to have " the genuine ring of the best days of minstrelsy," and many others, " fine old ballads," spoiled though they are more or less by tradition : we are told of them all that " the author counts for nothing ! "

We may, however, be reminded of another statement of Professor Child, that ballads are at their best when " the transmission has been purely through the mouths of unlearned people." But even if this be true, it is so only in a limited, a mnemonic, sense : also, only of the ballad of tradition can it be true ; and that it is so is by no means certain. Many of the ballads of Denmark have been preserved in the tradition of ladies ; and so have a few of the old songs and some of the old ballads of Scotland ; and while, in this tradition, they are certainly superior as literature, they probably accord more with the original than when they have passed through the mouths of unlearned people. True, unlearned people have limited powers of invention ; unlearned tradition is also sometimes tenacious of the general gist of the story, for it is the story that specially appeals to it ; and there are some remarkable instances of stanzas being apparently preserved, during many generations, in one tradition —whether wholly unlearned or not—which have been lost in another. But unlearned tradition evidently indulges in inventions of a sort. Generally, also, it is very careless as to expression and rhyme, or rather it tends to make the ballad "popular," in the sense of being mean and common and rude in style, and "impersonal," destitute of the traces of individual authorship, for the simple reason that it has been gradually remoulded by the processes of instinctively stupid interference with the original text, by the ignorant touches of those by whom it has during many generations been preserved, by their inevitable preference for their own colloquial and, in a literary sense, obtuse method of expression, and the generally prosy and jejune, and often confused character of their notions and sentiments.

Thus to say of a ballad that it is "truly popular in style" is a somewhat ambiguous eulogy. While it is to a ballad's advantage not to have been sophisticated by the deliberate improvements of the learned or the poetic editor, it is also to its detriment to have passed through the crucible of unlearned generations ; and the "truly popular in style" of tradition, may sometimes be very unlike the "truly popular in style" of the original ballad. Moreover, we have been told by Child, in the words of Mr Hart, that "a whole ballad may even be completely derived from print, and yet, in the course of time, revert to the popular form." But the popular form here referred to is not the form of the

original ballad before it passed through the hands
of the poetaster and became a broadside : it is
merely the popular traditional form. And, further,
if tradition possesses the power of causing printed
verse to assume a " popular form," it must be very
difficult to tell what has been the original character of
any lyric-epic or any piece of narrative verse, which
has happened in the course of time to have assumed
the form of a ballad " truly popular in style."

A more distinct reason than is to be found in any
of Child's statements, for the opinion that the author
counts for nothing is given by Professor Kittredge
in his introduction to the popular edition of Child's
" Ballads," Boston, 1904. " The extant ballads of
England and Scotland represent," he says, " the
end of a process, of which the beginning may not
improbably be discovered in the period of communal composition. They were not themselves
composed in this way, but were in the first instance
the work of individual authors, at least in the
majority of cases." These statements, ostensibly,
contain little of a very definite kind that one would
be disposed to dispute. Much depends on the
sequel, on the interpretation of them, for they do
not fully explain themselves. But he goes on to
explain : " These authors, however, were not
professional poets or minstrels, but members of the
folk." How does he · know ? Further he says :

" His subject is not his own—it belongs to the folk. It is a popular tradition of immemorial antiquity, or a situation so simple and obvious as to be a matter of general experience, or a recent occurrence which has been taken up by the mouth of common fame.   He has no wish to treat the theme in a novel way—no desire to utter his peculiar feelings about it or to impress it with his individuality."   That may be so, but there is a stupid and clever, an impressive and unimpressive method, of telling a story ; the first aim of the balladist is to be impressive and he cannot be so without the exercise of individual skill and art.   " The greatest ballads," says Professor Gummere, " affect us, not by the story itself, but by the way in which the story is told."   But, according to Professor Kittredge, the balladist " takes no credit to himself, for he deserves none.   What he does, many of his neighbours could do as well.   Accordingly he is impersonal and without self-consciousness." How modest and retiring must even village bards have been in the olden time !   But is such impersonality as it originally possesses not due to the character of its art, to the fact that it is a swift dramatic presentation of an episode ?   Again, even if the author be one of the folk, be, so to say, an amateur, might he not, after all, be somewhat cleverer than his neighbours ?   Why this dead level of ability and accomplishment ?   And why trouble about the productions of authors, which are so poor and common that they deserve no credit for them ?

" Further," says Professor Kittredge, " his composition is not a solitary act. He improvises, orally, with his audience before him—or rather about him. There is the closest emotional contrast between him and his hearers—a contact which must have a distinct effect on the composer, so that the audience, even if they kept silence (as they can hardly be supposed to do), would still have a kind of share in the poetic act. There is the strongest contrast to the situation of the modern literary artist, who, in the solitude of his study," etc., etc. " And the difference, it will be observed, consists in the part which the throng (the " folk ") performs—by its mere presence if nothing more—in the production (the " authorship ") of ballad poetry." But surely it is not incumbent that verse for an audience, verse to be sung even with a chorus, should be improvised, any more than it is incumbent that music to be danced should be improvised during the dance—in fact, if of any merit, it could not be so improvised. Professor Kittredge, then, goes on to tell us how " the audience will have a far larger share than that of sympathetic and stimulative emotional contact with the author." " As he composes, the author draws freely on a large stock of commonplaces which are public property. These

are, of course, entirely familiar to every person in
the company, as well as the points in any narrative
(for these are also fixed by long standing tradition)
at which the conventional stanzas must come in.
When the author arrives at such a point, the audience
join their voices with his.   So also in passages which
merely repeat, in identical terms, what has already
been said or sung, as in the delivery of a message.
Again, in a succession of stanzas constructed on
the principle of incremental repetition, the author
and the audience may become merged in the same
way, even if the first stanza of the series is in some
degree original.   Thus we have arrived at a state of
things which is in effect scarcely to be distinguished
from the supposedly inconceivable phenomenon of
a numerous throng composing poetry with one
voice."   One might almost suppose that Professor
Kittredge had seen the ballad factories of the
ancient village communities in full operation !   No
doubt all the premises being granted, and granted
exactly as stated, something approaching the sur-
prising conclusion is inevitable.   But the premises,
when one begins to examine them, soon grow to be
as great a marvel as the corollary.   What especially
is taken for granted is that the " author " has a
large stock of ballad commonplaces to draw upon,
even before the first ballad has been made.   It is
premised that the commonplaces—which, as matter

of fact, have been disseminated broadcast among ballads by the processes of tradition—were commonplace from the beginning, and formed a kind of support round which the ivy of the new material, such as it was, could twine itself in very much an instinctive and almost mechanical fashion, so that any author and any audience could between them manufacture ballads *ad infinitum*, ballads almost as alike as pins. But all ballads are not fashioned on the model of *The Hangman's Tree*, which he elects to use as his illustration. It is, perhaps, the most defective, if not the most distorted, version of *The Maid Freed from the Gallows* (95), all the English versions of which are, in the opinion of Child, " defective and distorted." But even of this Americanised version, Professor Kittredge tells us, " the audience are silent for the first two stanzas, and until the first stanza of the third is uttered," that is practically until the ballad, such as it is in this fractional fragment of a version, has been composed ! The remainder of the verses, being identical with what has gone before, but for the mention of new names—" mother," " sister," " sweetheart " or anything else *ad libitum*, to the selection of which the unanimous " throng " would require to be guided by the " author "—the only intellectual call upon the audience was a call merely upon its memory. Have we, therefore, approached a single

step towards the realization of the " phenomenon
of a unanimous throng composing poetry with one
voice ? " Would it not be as true to say that the
" unanimous throng," which join in the chorus
of the music hall songs, " compose with one voice,"
the verses of the music hall " stars ? "

The *Hangman's Tree*, Professor Kittredge admits
to be " an extreme instance of simplicity in plot and
of inevitableness in both structure and diction."
One is not so sure about the diction : the notion
of a father " riding through the air " would be
more conceivable now than in the times of old.
But even so, improvised or not, on his own showing
it is, though amounting to almost as little as it
could amount to and still express anything, the
" author's " very own ; the audience added nothing
to it whatever ; the " unanimous throng " were
not responsible for even a syllable of it.

Having set out with the professed purpose of
giving us a " typical instance " of individual authorship, he selects instead, as will be observed, an
exceptional instance which he, again, without
warning, transforms into a case of communal
authorship, or as near this as can even by him be
conceived ; and now these things achieved, he
winds up by declaring :—" Such a description is in
general warranted by the evidence ; and though
it cannot be proved of any of the English and

Scottish ballads it is not improbable for some of them." How can a description be in general warranted by the evidence, if it cannot be proved even in a single case ? Then, having reached this very negative conclusion, he goes on to say :— " It makes no difference whether a given ballad was, in fact, composed in the manner described, or whether it was composed (or even written) in solitude, provided the author belonged to the folk, derived his opinion from popular sources, made his ballad under the inherited influence of the method described, and gave it to the folk as soon as he had made it, and provided, moreover, the folk accepted the gift and subjected it to that course of oral tradition which " . . . " is essential to the production of a genuine ballad." Apparently, then, the unanimmous throng can after all be quite dispensed with in the original production of the ballad ; its composition may be " a solitary act " ; only the audience, waiting probably at the author's study door, must get hold of it at once, lest, on second thoughts he should seek " to impress it with his individuality." On one page Professor Kittredge says that it matters everything that the ballad should be improvised in presence of a throng, on another he says it matters nothing, provided the author imitates one that is made in this way. But how is he to get his model, since by the nature of the case no ballad can be known to him which has not been subjected to a course of oral tradition ?   Also, if oral tradition be necessary to the production of a genuine ballad, then clearly even *The Hangman's Tree*, whatever it may have been originally, could not have been produced, as it now is, in the manner described by Professor Kittredge.

On this point of oral tradition the opinion of Professor Kittredge is the antithesis of Child's. Child affirmed, and affirming, regretted that in tradition, even in the best of it, the ballad departs from the original form.   Professor Kittredge holds, on the contrary, that for " the production of a genuine ballad " oral tradition is " hardly second in importance to the original creative act."   This wonderful species of verse cannot, in his opinion, be produced by an individual " author," aided even by a communal throng of choralists.   Whatever it may be after production by " the original creative act," it is not properly a ballad until it has been subjected to " a course of oral tradition " ; though how many years, generations, or epochs is necessary to make it properly a ballad he does not state.

The speculations and illustrations of Professor Gummere in *The Beginnings of Poetry*, *The Popular Ballad*, and elsewhere, are in various ways suggestive. His theory of ballad authorship is pretty similar to that of Professor Kittredge ; but he connects the

ballad more definitely with the dance and with
the " rude chants," which are " the source of poetry
itself." To begin with, he, like Professor Kittredge,
" rules the minstrel out of court." Child, on the
contrary—who does not touch on the association
of the ballad with the dance or choral throng—
seems to imply that ballads were the work of a
fraternity whose business it was to furnish tales and
songs for the amusement of all classes of the people.
Of *The Lochmaben Harper* (192) he also says it has
" the genuine ring of the best days of minstrelsy " ,
and he describes *The Rising in the North* (175) as
" the work of a loyal but unsympathetic minstrel."
True, he refers to *Crow and Pie* (111),in the Rawlinson
MS. of the early sixteenth century, as " not a purely
popular ballad, but rather of the kind which for
convenience may be called a minstrel ballad." It
may be that *Crow and Pie* has nothing to do with
minstrelsy ; the old Scottish poets wrote verses of
the very same kind ; and several pieces very similar
to it are in the Bannatyne MS., and doubtless it
would have had a more decidedly " popular " form,
had it come to us through oral tradition. But,
avowedly, Child here used the word minstrel in a
special sense ; he probably referred to that variety
of minstrel who frequented the dwellings of the
upper classes ; and he probably had in his mind
that variety of ballad of which he wrote : " Nothing,

in fact, is more obvious than that many of the
ballads of the now most refined nations had their
origin in that class whose acts and fortunes they
depict—the upper class—though the growth of
civilization has driven them from the memory of
the highly polished and instructed, and has left
them as an exclusive possession of the uneducated."
Of *The Boy and the Mantle* (29), *King Arthur and
King Cornwall* (30), and *The Marriage of Sir Gawain*
(31) he also wrote : "They would come down by
professional rather than domestic tradition, through
minstrels rather than knitters or weavers. They
suit the hall better than the bower, the tavern or
public square better than the cottage, and would
not go to the spinning-wheel at all." Ballads for
the delectation of the upper classes could hardly
be improvised with the aid of unanimous throngs ;
nor apparently did Child contemplate this possibility
in the case of any kind of ballad. Moreover, ballads
constructed by the folk, in accordance with the
Kittredge-Gummere theory, would suit the public
square better than the cottage ; and would go
better to the accompaniment of the harp or viol
than the spinning-wheel or the weaver's shuttle.

In ruling the minstrel out of court, Professor
Gummere adopts, as his own, the peremptory
method of Professor Kittredge, who does it by the
following proposition :—" It is capable of practically

F

formal proof that for the last two or three centuries,
the English and Scottish ballads have not, as a
general thing, been sung and transmitted by professional minstrels or their representatives.   There
is no reason whatever for believing that the state
of things between 1300 and 1600 was different in
this regard from that between 1600 and 1900, and
there are many reasons for believing that it was
not different." But (1) surely the introduction
of printing made, alone, an immense difference
between the earlier and the later periods ; (2)
Professor Kittredge himself, almost immediately
afterwards, tells us that minstrels had a share in
carrying ballads from place to place ; (3) ballads
in early times could hardly find their way into
widely remote parts of the country except by
minstrels ; and (4) minstrels and " their representatives " gradually ceased to exist during the
later period, but there is every reason to suppose
that in the seventeenth century and later, ballads
from Scotland found their way into England through
itinerant singers or reciters.   Indeed, Professor
Gummere himself makes mention of medieval
reciters—that is, professional reciters—if not actually composing ballads, altering them, or adding
to them.

But supposing we do rule the minstrel out of
court, have we no other option than to rule into

court the improvising village author and the unanimous throng, or, as Professor Gummere would put it, the improvising band of choral dancers ? By no means. In the days of Dante, as we have seen, verses to be danced were written by individual poets. The poet, minstrel or not, may have written them for the minstrel who sang them, while a chorus danced to the music which he sang and played ; or he may have written them for accomplished amateurs of the upper classes who could sing and play, and who sang them to be danced to by ladies. In his " Goldyn Targe," the Scottish poet, Dunbar —evidently founding on the customs of the time— represents the gods playing on harp or lute and singing " balletis with michty notis clere " while ladies " to dance full soberly assayit," and he distinguishes them from the " ballatis in lufe," which he represents the goddesses as singing, " as was the guise," that is, the fashion. These dance songs referred to by Dunbar as " balletis " may, or may not, have been the lyric-epics now known as ballads ; but if not, they must have been *caroles* of some kind ; and we hear of the existence of the *carole* before we hear of the existence of what is now known as the popular ballad. True, Professor Kittredge tells us that nobody doubts that the Angles and Saxons had ballads in abundance when they invaded Britain ; but, in fact, a great many people doubt this ; and even Professor Gummere affirms that " to claim for this old period ballads of the kind common since the fifteenth century in England, Scandinavia and Germany is an assertion impossible to prove." And while this is so, it is not in the least difficult to prove that the *carole* existed during this older period. Professor Gummere himself even records—what is otherwise well known —that high born folk loved the *carole* and sang it as they danced. Further he says—and this again is also common knowledge—that these *caroles* had the common choral features of repetition and refrain. So that there is, to say the least, a possibility—indeed various evidence seems to make it as nearly as possible a certainty—that the narrative ballad borrowed from the *carole* the choral features of repetition and refrain. But while unable to discover anything like the ballad as we now have it in the older period, he yet tells us that the exulting song of Miriam and the women after the miraculous passage of the Red Sea, and the congratulatory song of the women who met David as he returned from the slaughter of the Philistines were improvised ballads. On the contrary, in the first case Miriam is represented merely as asking the women to sing a song of thanksgiving and praise to God : " Sing ye to the Lord for he hath triumphed gloriously." Then all that Holy Writ represents the women as singing in praise of David is :—" Saul hath slain his thousands and David his tens of thousands." This, we are told, " is popular refrain ; and the narrative improvisation can be inferred." On the contrary, this is evidently what may be termed the theme of the *carole* and the popular refrain may be inferred. It seems, in fact, to have been an exulting, exclamatory song like the Bannockburn one already quoted (p. 2), where the refrain happens to have been preserved.

Again Professor Gummere will have it that Cnut's song, of which all that is preserved is :—

> " Merie sungen the muneches binnen Ely
> Tha knut ching [King] reu thaerbye ;
> Roweth knites, noer the land,
> And here we thes muneches saeng " ;

he will have it that this " is the beginning of recorded English balladry ; but it is balladry from the warrior caste, and of the chronicle or epic type " : it is also " the first glimpse of actual ballad structure and the ballad's metrical form." That it is the first glimpse of rhyme may be admitted, but the glimpse probably belongs to the twelfth century, and about 150 years after the death of Cnut. Indeed Professor Gummere himself says " one accepts the picture "—the picture of improvisation—" as true, while doubting the authenticity of the frag-

ment " ; and again he says, " its story of origin is
obviously conventional and based upon surmise."
Not only so, but he tells us : " Of the song itself
there is so little left that little can be inferred " ;
but why, therefore, infer that it is balladry, and not
only so, but even " balladry from the warrior caste
and of the chronicle or epic type ? "

According to Professor Gummere the original
ballad—which at first is only epical, so to speak,
in the germ—is necessarily improvised. In *The
Popular Ballad* he defines it generally " as a narrative
lyric made and sung at the dance, and handed
down in popular tradition " ; but this statement,
he tells us, requires further explication and the
explication is :—" The making of the original
ballad is a choral dramatic process and treats a
situation ; the traditional course of the ballad is
really an epic process which tends more to treat a
series of events as a story."   In his article on the
ballad in *The Cambridge History of English Literature*,
Vol. II., he is still more specific :—" The structure
of the ballad—what makes it a species, the elements
of it—derives from choral and dramatic conditions ;
what gives it its peculiar art of narrative is the epic
process working by oral tradition and gradually
leading to a new structure, with choral and dramatic
elements, still surviving though dwindling, in the
traces of refrain and incremental repetition."

Interpreted in one way it is possible to agree with a good deal of this. The earlier ballads, sung probably to the dance, or at least made to be sung with choral effects, are more concentrated, more dramatic, less detailed than the later ones or those not meant to be so sung. In the course of tradition ballads may also be almost transformed both by addition and subtraction, and even by conjunction with other ballad narratives ; and, in any case, there are ballads which are more dramatic in their form than others. But evidently Professor Gummere means much more than this. Going a step further than Professor Kittredge, he asserts, in the first place, that the ballad never has an existence except by improvisation, and generally improvisation in the presence of, and mainly by, a dancing throng. Evidently, to be so improvised, its epic or narrative character must be reduced to a minimum ; its statements, if the dancing throng be more responsible for them than any definite individual, could hardly be other than commonplace, if even so much as that. In the case, however, of a legend it would appear that the dancing throng, moved by a common instinct or inspiration, change it on the spur of the moment into a dramatic something or other, destitute of story or narrative, and that it again becomes a story—the same old legend, it would appear, in several cases, that it was before—through the processes of tradition.

As a proof that it is actually done in this way, he refers again and again to the fisher ballads of the Faroes. But (1) the Faroe fisher ballads were evidently fashioned in rude imitation of the better class ballads; without the introduction of the foreign fashion into the Faroes they would have had no existence; (2) there is no evidence that they were improvised in the manner asserted by Professor Gummere and became epical by augmenting and transforming tradition; (3) they are very woeful specimens of verse, and of interest only from their touching and almost childish naïvete; and (4) they are not sung to native melodies of ancient fisher tradition or of new fisher improvisation, but to lugubrious tunes, borrowed, according to Thuren, from the Protestant Psalmody. Thus they do not help in the least to make credible Professor Gummere's theory of improvisation; they serve only to show what a wide gulf would separate ballads made, in whatever fashion, by the folk from even the average ballad of tradition. On the other hand, this theory of the old form of the ballad hardly distinguishes it from the rudest and simplest forms of the *Carole*. According to such a theory we might even suppose the possibility, and, indeed, the likelihood that the Bannockburn song, which treats—rudely enough, but what else could you expect from improvising army minstrels ? —a situation in a dramatic fashion, becoming in the course of time a detailed story and a real traditional ballad.

Having got his ballad improvised, Professor Gummere then tells us how it becomes epical, that is how it assumes its narrative form ; for be it observed, he does not mean merely that ballads of a late period are generally more epical, more detailed in their narrative than the earlier ones ; he means that in its original form no ballad is detailed. And the reason why he must mean this is that he has ruled the minstrel out of court, and with the minstrel any individual who could be epical. From beginning to end, from its earlier to its later years, and through all the stages of its strange—may we not say well nigh miraculous ?—development, the ballad in his opinion is the creation of the folk, of the folk in the collective sense : in the first instance of a choral throng, and in the end, if there be an end, of a long traditional folk process. Few ballads he tells us can remain in their initial stage. How, on his theory, could any ballad remain in this stage ? This is how he describes the process : " They are submitted to oral tradition and are sung as stories rather than presented as action. More than this, a whole narrative, often a definite occurrence, historical or legendary, or even, it may be, a late form of some old classical tale will find its way into the structure and so be handed down in the traditional way." It will thus be seen that in his opinion, once a ballad has been, so to speak, dramatised from some legend or story by a choral throng, the choral throng ceases to have anything further to do with it; it passes into tradition and again becomes a story, but apparently a new variety of story. The choral throng, however, leave it to its fate, and begin improvising another ballad, or the germ of another ballad, to be again perfected by the traditional process, and so on, and so on. But may we not rather suppose that the real vogue of the ballad was during the generations when it was presented in dramatic form by a singer and choral throngs, not when it ceased to be produced in this way, and began to be known merely as a traditional ballad? No, by no means! The ballad, we are told, differs from every other species of literature in that the choral throng merely, so to speak, conceive and bear it. Its development towards its proper maturity proceeds long after the choral throngs, that have brought it forth and nourished its infancy, have ceased to be. For they have endowed it, if not with an actual living spirit, with a wonderful parasitical proclivity, otherwise unknown in literature, by virtue of which it is able to absorb into its being " a whole narrative, often a definite occurrence historical or legendary, or even it may be a late form of some old classical tale." If this be " the last word on the subject," there is, of course, to quote again M. Jeanroy, " nothing more to be done but reverently to bow down before the mysterious agency of nature." But previous to doing so, the reader may as well take into consideration that Professor Gummere must, for example, according to his theory hold, and indeed actually states, that " the very old ballad *Robyn and Gandeleyn* " has come to be what it is by this double folk process. What the singer proceeds to tell is, he says, not his own story at all. When he says he heard " a carpynge of a clerk," that is " the story of a bookman, a scholar, an authority "; the reader must bear in mind that the minstrel is barred ; but surely a bookman-singer is rather an anomaly. But, however that may be, what he tells is not anything of his : it is " a genuinely popular and traditional ballad with its refrain." Any one who chooses to believe that the genius of the improvising throng and the chance of blind tradition are, together, sufficient to account for the production of this fine ballad, may be left in the possession of his conviction : my own mental faculties will not permit me to conceive its possibility.

As regards the question when ballads came into

vogue, one thing is beyond doubt, that the oldest
surviving ballads of every country are of later date
than the old epic verse. In Scandinavia and
Britain the ballad is first associated not with the
old native alliterative blank verse, but with stanzas
in rhyme having internal refrains after the manner
of the old French *caroles* ; and, in addition, there is
in Scandinavia evidence of borrowing from the older
epical sources. Some of the Scandinavian ballads
dealing with the old historical traditions are merely
re-readings of older epic poems, in a new, a lyric-
epic or dramatic-epic form. Then the French
carole dances, with the French tunes and refrains,
did not come into vogue in Scandinavia and Britain
until the twelfth century, and were not until at
least the next century, so far as existing evidence
points, used for lyric-epic verse ; while in the case
of the ballad in France and the Latin countries the
weight of evidence seems to show that it did not
exist there earlier than the fifteenth century. It
is thus at least possible that the lyric-epic, now
known in England as the ballad, was the creation
of the Scandinavians ; but in France and the Latin
countries there may well have been similar influences
favouring this species of literary development,
though it may have come later. But, in any case,
it seems more likely that the ballad had an independent beginning in Scandinavia than that it

came there, along with the French *carole*, from the
English and Scottish Danes who got it from France.
The only really feasible evidence of an early ballad
connection between Britain and Denmark is found
in *Earl Brand*, which, on account of a certain similarity of rhyme in one particular place, it has been
surmised Denmark got from the British Danes as
early as the twelfth century. But, at the best, this
is a very sandy foundation on which to build such
a cardinal theory. *Prima facie*, it is more probable
that the British Danes got it from Denmark, but
the likelihood is against either theory. However
old may be the Danish historical ballad, it is certain
that there are no historical ballads in Britain so
old even as the thirteenth century. They may,
though it is unlikely, have existed : that is not the
question here ; but since at least they have not
survived, the survival of this solitary ballad in
Scotland not only from the twelfth century, but
very much as it was then, is the reverse of probable.
Then there is, besides, the difficulty of the weight of
evidence being against the existence at so early
a date of the lyric-epic amongst the French ; and in
addition the very slight character of the ballad
connection between Britain and Denmark as regards
ballad themes and the much wider relations between
Denmark and France, seem to show that Britain's
ballad connection with Denmark was of late origin

and that she owes more to Denmark than Denmark owes to her. The connection may have begun with the marriage of James III. to Margaret of Denmark, from which time the relations between Scotland and Denmark became exceptionally intimate, and it may have been augmented with the marriage of the learned and poetic James VI. to the Danish Princess Anne; while it is further by no means impossible that several Scottish versions of Danish ballads have been derived from Danish broadsides.

The difficulty of course remains to explain the close literary connection between Scandinavia and the French and other Latin nations as regards the *carole* and the ballad; but it is not solved by the supposition that the French ballad, is, as well as the *carole*, of earlier date than the Danish ballad; we have still to explain the closeness of the connection. It cannot be explained on the theory that it began with the English Danes of the twelfth century. The thread of connection is too slight to explain the presence of so many French themes—derived apparently from romances and tales—in the Danish ballads. It would almost seem as if they were utilized for this purpose by the Danes before they were so used by the French, and that the French also utilized them later, on their own account. As for the late origin of the ballads in France and the Latin countries, it is difficult to resist the repre-

sentations of Gaston Paris. He has shown very
clearly the difference in form and style between
the lyric-epic ballad and the purely epic poetry
of the *Chanson de Geste* which flourished in France
from the ninth until the twelfth century; and
he has further pointed out that none of the heroes
of the French epic verses have been the subject of
any lyric-epic verse that has been preserved. In
Scandinavia as in France and in France as in
Scandinavia, the lyric-epic is evidently of later
date than the epic *chanson*, or the purely lyrical
carole. It seems to have originated in a kind of
fusion of the two styles of poetry; but whether its
original source was France or Denmark there is as
yet no conclusive evidence to show.

In any case the lyric-epic did not originate
amongst what is usually termed the folk; it neither
had its origin in individual peasant authorship, nor
was it the creation of dancing throngs of the
rural variety. As we have seen, Professor Gummere
records that high-born folk loved the *carole* and sang
it as they danced, and in such high fashion were
dance songs either of the *carole* or of the lyric-epic
type in the time of Dunbar, that he represents the
singing of them, accompanied with the harp or lute,
as a fit relaxation of the Gods, while ladies danced
to their music and their sentiment or their story.
Also Professor Child, for all the respect paid by him

to the tradition of the unlearned, affirmed that " the ballad is not originally the product or the property of the common orders of the people " ; and it is certain that in Denmark it was fostered and favoured more particularly by the upper classes, and was for some centuries the chief medium of the nations literary expression and culture. To be preserved mainly in the traditions of the common people, can therefore hardly be reckoned its just or appropriate fate. It has been its misfortune rather than its felicity. Its traditional development, in this fashion, could not possibly be other than decadent ; it was beyond it to produce anything that could properly be regarded as a new literary creation, but only a kind of mongrel debasement.

CHAPTER IV

THE LATER BRITISH BALLADS

THE lyrical, condensed, and dramatic ballads are the more vivid and poetic, and evidence a higher art than the longer recitals. Probably they are also of earlier origin, and the precursors of the other variety. During what may be termed the golden age of balladry—it seems to have had a golden age at least in Denmark—they were specially favoured by the upper classes, and may well have been sung in the halls of the castles with harp accompaniment by accomplished minstrels, whilst the ladies danced to their music and sentiment with appropriate gestures. The longer ballad— which, it would appear, was also sometimes danced —though occasionally marked by poetic touches and often graphic in narrative, is usually very much a mere rhymed tale, dependent for its effect rather on the clever presentation of details than the cumulative dramatic climax. This variety is of considerable antiquity. *Robin Hood and the Monk*, preserved in a Cambridge MS. of about 1450, is ninety stanzas long, and *Robin Hood and the Potter*, in a MS. of about 1500, runs to eighty-three. Both

G

seem intended for recital—possibly in a kind of half-chanting style — to an audience ; and they might well be recited in very effective fashion by one skilled in the antique professional methods. Here and there they contain phrases which point to their recital by an individual before a merely listening audience. Thus *Robin Hood and the Monk* ends :—

> " God, that is ever a crownèd king,
>   Bring us all to his bliss."

And *Robin Hood and the Potter*, after a stanza which condenses the opening stanzas of the other ballad—the two ballads may well have had the same author—begins the second stanza :—

> " Herkens, god yeman,
>   Comley, corteys and god "—

and the ballad ends :—

> " God haffe mersey on Robyn Hodys solle,
>   And saffe all god yemanry."

Both, after their own fashion, are very spirited pieces ; but that fashion is not strictly lyrical or dramatic. They are quite different in style, for example, from *The Jolly Pinder of Wakefield* (124), meant evidently to be sung ; and its original, from which the black-letter version was derived, may

well have been an excellent ballad of the older
dramatic type. As the ballad ceased to be associated with the dance, the longer recital tended to
become more prevalent, and the shorter form became more lyrical, so that it often becomes difficult
to make any definite distinction between a ballad
and a song. Good examples of these later song-
ballads are *The Bonnie House o' Airlie* (199), *Johny
Faa or the Gypsy Laddie* (200), *The Bonnie Earl
of Murray* (181)—probably, however, touched by
Ramsay—and *Bonnie James Campbell* (210), all
of Scottish origin. The mere fact, also, that with
the introduction of printing, ballads came to be
perused in private as well as listened to in public,
tended to modify their form.

Gradually the old half-mythical romantic themes
and tales of wonder ceased to be utilized by the
balladist. The later ballads, long or short, are
mainly historical—either of a chronicle character,
or commemorative of a famous incident or event,
or concerned with the setting forth of recent
calamities and deeds of terror. Some of the earlier
British historical ballads, *Chevy Chase, Otterbourne*,
etc., have been referred to in chapter ii. (p. 54).
Few old British historical ballads survive, though
there is abundant evidence, especially in Scotland,
that ballad versions of events have done much to
colour the narrative of the older historians, and in

several cases they seem to be the source of representations of incidents and events now proved to be erroneous. It is more than likely, for example, that the evidently invented details about the execution of William, sixth Earl of Douglas, and his brother David, in Edinburgh Castle in 1440, were derived from a ballad, which possibly may have included the lines quoted by Hume of Godscroft :—

> " Edinburgh Castle, towne and tower,
>   God grant thou sink for sinne !
> And that even for the black dinner
>   Earl Douglas gat therein."

It is also a more than feasible hypothesis that the *Chronicle* of Lyndsay of Pitscottie derives much of its picturesqueness of detail, with its more than occasional travesty of facts, from ballad narratives, as, for example, the highly dramatic and circumstantial description of the execution of Cochrane, the favourite of James III., at Lauder Bridge, the vivid account of the Duke of Albany's escape from Edinburgh Castle, and of the flight of James III. from Sauchieburn and his murder at Milton Mill, and the records of the feats of Sir Andrew Wood ; while it is certain that the details of the story of Johnnie Armstrong are either borrowed from the ballad or *vice versâ*.

Neither of the surviving ballads on the Battle of

Harlaw (1411) can be contemporaneous with the battle ; but it is possible that that in the French octave, preserved in Ramsay's *Tea Table Miscellany*, and of which there was at one time a broadside copy, has—though rejected by Child, because " it is not in the least of a popular character "—a direct connexion with the ballad mentioned in *The Complaynt of Scotland*. In any case it is older than *The Battle of Harlaw* (163), printed by Child, the comparatively recent character of which is sufficiently indicated by its jocular imitation of Highland Scots ; and, indeed, the latter may well have been the work of Dougal Graham, the Glasgow bellman.

King Henry Fifth's Conquest of France (164) may not be of earlier date than the broadside versions ; but *Sir John Butler* (165) and the figurative *Rose of England* (166), both in the Percy MS., preserve something of the antique style, the latter being also slightly alliterative. A few commemorate events in the reign of Henry VIII. They include *Sir Andrew Barton*, already referred to ; *The Death of Queen Jane* (170), the broadside origin of which seems to be indicated by the meanly vulgar character of the fragmentary, traditional versions that survive ; *Thomas Cromwell* (171), of which there are only a few halting stanzas, preserved in the Percy MS., and two celebrating, respectively, the English victories of Flodden and Pinkie Cleugh. *Flodden Field* (168), which Thomas Deloney included in his *Pleasant History of John Winchcombe,* first published in 1597, as " made by the commons of England," might well have been mainly Deloney's own.   At anyrate its real antiquity is not so certain, nor its literary interest so great, as those of the alliterative ode preserved in the Lyme MS. and published in the Chetham *Miscellany,* vol. ii.   Here we have a kind of *Chanson de Geste,* penned, it would appear, by one present at the fight.   It concludes :—

> " For all the lords of their land were left them behind :
> Besides Branxton, in a brook, breathless they lie,
> Gaping against the moon their ghosts went away."

Accidentally saved, evidently very much as it was originally made, from the general literary wreck of old verse, this *Chanson* may serve to show how imperfect is our knowledge of ancient English and Scottish minstrelsy, and how unsafe it is to indulge in dogmatic inferences from the largely transmogrified specimens that have been preserved in tradition, or in the travesties of broadside poetasters.   *Musselburgh Field* (172), the fragment on the later battle, preserved in the Percy MS., and the first line of which is quoted by Sir Toby in *Twelfth Night,* is, if not the work of an eye-witness of the battle, that of one pretty well informed about its details, the description of the terror of the Highlanders when they heard the sound of the artillery being in exact accordance with fact. It is in stanzas of double rhymes, and differs considerably in style from a later and very poor English ballad, *Earl Bothwell* (174), also preserved in the Percy MS., and in its surviving form probably the work of a London broadsidist.

As for *Mary Hamilton* (173), Mr Andrew Lang has disposed of the theory that it might relate to a Miss Hamilton, maid of honour to the Empress Catherine, wife of Peter the Great ; but although a " Mademoiselle Hamilton, fille du gouverneur d'Ecosse," was in attendance on Mary Stuart in France, she was not one of the four Mary's—none of Arran's daughters were named Mary ; and is not known to have been involved in a scandal of the kind alluded to in the ballad. Scott, who first published it, suggested that it referred to the case of a French waiting-woman who, as recorded by Knox, had a child to the Queen's French apothecary, and who, also, with the apothecary, was hanged in the public street of Edinburgh for its murder. Knox further relates : " What bruit the Maries and the rest of the dancers had, the ballads of that age do witness which we for modesty's sake omit ; " but the ballads alluded to were evidently scurrilous, satirical ballads of Edinburgh versifiers. They could have borne no resemblance whatever to the semi-sentimental *Mary Hamilton* ballad. Moreover, all the supposed complete, all the more than fragmentary, versions of this ballad are very corrupt, and largely a patch-work assortment from other ballads. Burns, for example, in a letter to Mrs Dunlop, 27th January 1790, quotes the stanzas: "Little did my mother think," from an old Scottish ballad which he does not further designate, but surely would have done, had it been a ballad referring to a waiting-woman of the Queen of Scots; and, that the ballad he quoted did not refer to a poor ruined female is further implied in his statement that this was the subject of the next ballad he goes on to quote. It is, however, possible that the stanza beginning, "Last night there were four Maries," is substantially authentic and ancient. It may well have been a variation on one belonging to a satirical ballad on the hasty marriage of Mary Livingstone to John Semple; and, indeed, some versions have stanzas representing the queen going to Edinburgh or Glasgow, "a rich wedding for to see," and in-congruously bringing with her the doomed waiting-woman, so finely arrayed that the people "in every town" took her for the queen! The publica-tion in the first edition of the *Minstrelsy* of a frag-ment of three stanzas only, seems, also, to have had not a little to do with the production of the com-plete versions, some of them with borrowed and choicely mangled stanzas like the following :—

> " ' Cast off, cast off my gown,' she said,
>   ' But let my petticoat be ;
>   And tye a napkin on my face
>   For that gallows I downa see ' "—

which is evidently a kind of parody reminiscence of one in *The Laird of Wariston* (194), referring, appropriately enough, to a case of burning at the stake.

The bulk of the later British ballads deal with Border feuds or forays, or with deeds of lawlessness in the Scottish Lowlands or Highlands, or with episodes in the Stewart risings. The English rebellion of the Earls of Northumberland and Westmoreland, in 1570, is commemorated in three ballads preserved in the Percy MS., *The Rising in the North* (175), *Northumberland betrayed by Douglas* (176), and *The Earl of Westmoreland* (177). All three represent minstrelsy in its decadence, and a very deteriorated form of the long recital compared with the Robin Hood ballads. Certain of the English ballads relating Border frays or feuds, though homely and halting in expression, yet possess a certain rude force and actuality, lacking in the ballads now mentioned. *The Rookhope Ryde* (179) reveals in its very prosy, matter-of-fact style, the dauntless, self-reliant attitude of the hardy Borderers towards their hazardous and precarious circumstances. *The Death of Parcy Reed* (193) is, notwithstanding its woeful lapses of rhyme, in essence even a superior production. It is a very vivid and dramatic sketch of treachery :—

> " O waken, O waken, Parcy Reed,
>   For we do doubt thou sleeps too long ;
>   For yonder's the five Crosiers coming,
>   They're coming by the Hingin Stane."

Hughie Grame (191), of which the recited versions are evidently derived from printed copies, is also, even in its exceedingly corrupt broadside form, at once effectively spirited and pathetic. A lyrical lament for the murder of William Aynsley of Shaftoe in Tynedale by the Scottish Rutherfords in 1598, was published by Professor C. H. Frith from the Ashmole MSS., in the *Scottish Historical Review* for July 1908. Though more in the lyrical than the ballad form, it is worthy of attention as a genuine specimen of the rhyming skill of, probably, the later English Border minstrel. The lament is put in the mouth of the murdered man's widow and begins :—

> " Lament, Ladyes, Lament,
>   Lament Northumberland,
> My Love is fra me rent,
>   Was doughty of his hand ;
> Forth i' the feyld faytinge,
>   The formast o' the chease,

> The Scote him slue by slyght,
> Myen ene [own] deare Loue, ah las !
>   Lere, Lere, ryng terre roe,
>   Lere, Lere, ryng terre roe,
>   La Lere, ryng terre roe ran,
>   O hone hone o riea.''

But by far the most notable specimen of the English Border Muse is *The Fray of Suport*, published in Scott's *Border Minstrelsy* but omitted in Child's collection. True, it is difficult to reconcile it with any form of the theory that the author of the ballad counts for nothing, or the communal throng plus tradition for everything ; but there is nothing in its form to prevent it being ranked, according to Professor Gummere's conception, as a ballad. It is even a ballad with a refrain, a really apposite and alive refrain ; it treats a situation if any ballad ever did ; and, in fact, it is a true Border ballad, and one of the most stirring and rousing ballads of the purely dramatic type :—

> '' Ah ! but they will play ye another jigg,
>   For they will out at the big rig,
>   And thro' at Fargy Grame's gap.
>   But I hae another wile for that :
>   For I hae little Will and stalwart Wat,
>   And lang Aicky in the Souter Moor,
>   Wi' his sleuth-dog sits in his watch right sure ;

Shou'd the dog gie a bark,
He'll be out in his sark,
And die or won.
    Fy lads, shout a' a' a' a' a',
    My gear's a ta'en."

But the ballads celebrating the exploits of the
Scottish reivers are superior—the above ballad
excepted—to the ballads emanating from the
English side of the Borders. Professor Gummere,
in *The Popular Ballad*, cites Mr Lang's interpretation
of a passage of Leslie's *History* as favouring the
communal or improvised origin of the Scottish
Border ballads. Leslie records that the Borderers
" delight in the songs which they themselves make
about the deeds of their ancestors, or the ingenious
methods of driving a prey." Professor Gummere
quotes the Latin, as more apposite than Dalrymple's
Scots translation, and adds : " This is unequivocal :
ipsi confingunt is plain talk. The Borderers, then,
made songs about their ancestors' raids and about
their own : so do primitive folk all over the world."
But Professor Gummere's own statement is not
unequivocal ; it seems to imply that the surviving
Border ballads represent a very primitive type of
verse—either a communal dance-song or an improvised lay of a fighting man ; but just before
this he tells us that they " must be put in a class far
advanced in narrative skill and scope beyond the

traditional domestic tale that best represents the
type." How possibly could verse by say, Johnnie,
or Willie, or Archie Armstrong, or Dick o' the Cow,
or the Red Rowan, or any other Border reiver you
like to name, be so far " advanced in narrative skill
and scope " ? Again, we are told by George
Buchanan of the Highland clans that " they had
songs celebrating the praises of brave men, their
bards seldom choosing any other subject." Now
Leslie states nothing to imply that the Borderers
did not, like the Highland clans, have bards of
their own ; and their condition was certainly not
more primitive than that of the Highlanders.
Further, whatever Mr Lang's earlier opinions about
the Borderers themselves making ballads might
amount to, he is now convinced that the bulk of the
surviving ballads belong to the seventeenth century,
and were made some time after the events they
celebrate, presumably by minstrels of some sort ;
so that Leslie's statement, interpreted as Professor
Gummere seeks to interpret it, could hardly apply
to them. True, we may have no specimens of the
songs to which Bishop Leslie refers ; and on what
does not now exist we can pass no judgment. Still
it is possible that *Johnnie Armstrong* (169), of much
the same type as the later ballads, was known to
Bishop Leslie, for unless we hold it to be a for-
gery from Lyndsay's *Chronicle,* it was known to

Lyndsay, a contemporary of Leslie. Again there is an English broadside, *John Armstrong's Good Night,* of about 1630, the very corruptness of which is proof of the existence of a Scottish version long anterior to it, and very similar to that which Ramsay affirms he wrote down from recital.

While vaguely attributing the Border ballads to " warriors who have the communal feeling," Professor Gummere is only able to cite one ballad to which this description might possibly apply. Of *The Lads of Wamphray* (184) he says : " It seems to spring straight from the fact ; and one is tempted here, if anywhere, to apply Bishop Leslie's *ipsi confingunt,* and to charge the making of the ballad to the very doers of the deed of revenge," which, being interpreted, must surely mean that he is not tempted to do so about any of the other Border ballads. But is there any reason whatever, except his own theory, why he should be tempted to attribute this very stirring and vivid ballad to the very doers of the deed of revenge ? Ostensibly it is not written by them but of them, and why then should we suppose that Willie o' the Kirkhill, assisted by the lads and lasses—very ignorant lads and lasses they were in those days—of Wamphray was the most likely author of this brilliant celebration of his feat ?

With much more reason might we attribute *The*

Fray of Suport to the spoiled English Borderer who is represented as raising the war-hoop on behalf of his stolen cattle ; and with equal reason might we apply it to *The Raid of Reidswire*, also in Scott's *Minstrelsy*, but omitted by Child as " not in the popular style." It is written in the French octave, and has not been popularized by traditional debasement, for, not long after the event it celebrates, it was copied out by Bannatyne in his MS. ; but it is undeniably a ballad, a ballad, also, displaying an intimate knowledge of the fight, and avowedly the work of one present at it :—

> " The swallow tail frae tackles flew,
>   Five hundreth flain into a flight,
>   But we had pestelets enew,
>   And shot among them as we might ;
>   With help of God the game gaed right,
>   Fra time the foremost of them fell ;
>   Then ower the know without good night,
>   They ran with mony a shout and yell."

It is not unlikely—indeed more than likely—that the Border ballads, *Jamie Telfer* (190), *Kinmont Willie* (186), *Dick o' the Cowe* (185), *Hobie Noble* (189), and *Archie of Ca' Field* (188), all dealing with incidents towards the close of the sixteenth century, and all in a peculiar lilt of their own, were by one and the same balladist. Topographical errors and variances with facts have been pointed out by different writers, including Mr Lang, who on this account is now disposed to assign them a considerably later date than the events they record ; but the blunders of current reports and the changes of tradition have to be taken into account.

Somewhat different in style from those six ballads —more polished and artful—is *The Lochmaben Harper* (192). *Lord Maxwell's Goodnight* (195), with the refrain, " But I may not stay with thee," is also in quite another vein ; and though *The Song of the Outlaw Murray* (305) somewhat resembles them, it may possibly be of earlier date and by another author.

The liberties taken by Scott with ballad texts has been the subject of elaborate discussion between Colonel the Hon. Fitzwilliam Elliot and Mr Andrew Lang.   Minute examination of the points at issue between them is here impossible.   Colonel Elliot's *notanda* are, in various respects, of considerable interest and value ; but Mr Lang, I think, has shown that his more extreme inferences against Scott derive from an imperfect acquaintance with the facts.   Had he, for example, examined the version of *Auld Maitland* which Hogg sent to Scott, and compared it with the *Minstrelsy* version, he could not have made the suggestion that " Scott himself assisted in the composition of *Auld Maitland*."   Apparently Scott brought himself to

believe—what he strongly wished to believe—that
the dreary and long-winded production procured for
him by Hogg had, " notwithstanding its present
appearance," a " claim to very high antiquity " ;
and the statement of Laidlaw seems to show that
some kind of ballad, termed *Auld Maitland,* was
known to Hogg's maternal grandfather. So far,
at least, it seems difficult—indeed impossible—not
to agree with Mr Lang ; but his vindication of
Hogg is not quite so convincing. True, he shows—
a cardinal point—that Hogg could not, as Colonel
Elliot supposes, obtain information of Maitland's
three sons (mentioned in a poem then, he says,
only in MS.) from Leyden ; but Scott might have
mentioned it to Laidlaw, though the fact is, it was
published in Pinkerton's *Ancient Scottish Poems*, 1786 !
Hogg said he copied the ballad from the recitation
of his uncle, corroborated by his mother. Later, his
mother—in proof of Hogg's good faith—recited it to
Scott, the whole sixty-five stanzas, Mr Lang thinks ;
but if she knew it so well as this, why did Hogg, in
the first instance, go to his uncle for it ? Then were
their versions exactly similar ? and if not, in what
way did Hogg construct the version sent to Scott ?
Further, Hogg states that his mother's memory of
many of her songs was " very much impaired " ;
but if that were so, how could she retain in it the
long and dull recitation termed *Auld Maitland* ?

H

Much of Colonel Elliot's futile speculations and conclusions about Scott's part in the preparation of his version of *Otterbourne*, can only be accounted for by his failure to consult the various versions printed in Child's edition.   Had he done this and read attentively Hogg's letters, he could hardly have formed the extreme conviction against Scott's good faith which Mr Lang has so carefully confuted. Still, it must be admitted that the eagerness of Scott to obtain " a complete Scottish Otterbourn " seems to have had a rather too stimulating effect on Hogg, and caused him to have recourse to methods which were confessedly ingenious ;   while Scott not only gave his imprimatur to Hogg's methods, so far as Hogg revealed them, but supplemented the ingenuity of Hogg with additional ingenuity of his own.   Avowedly, Hogg constructed his version of the death of Douglas out of the plain prose and lines and half lines of " a crazy old man and a woman   deranged   in   her   mind."   His   general method of recording from recital is, also, sufficiently indicated in his own remark :   " Sure no man will like   an   old   song   the   worse   of   being   somewhat harmonious."   With the aid of Hogg's version and lines or portions of lines from the Herd MS. and the Sharp MS., Scott constructed the three fine stanzas beginning—

" My wound is deep, I fain would sleep ;
   Take thou the vanguard of the three,
  And hide me by the braken bush
   That grows on yonder lilye lea."

The remarkable character of the literary feat, the wonderful transformation effected on the faltering reminiscences of the two crazy reciters by the two poetic conspirators—if the word conspirators can apply to such peculiar enthusiasts—is rather slurred over by Mr Lang ; but the result achieved being so excellent, one is naturally disposed to be more grateful than censorious.

In regard to the two purely Border ballads, *Kinmont Willie* and *Jamie Telfer*, there is more room for difference of opinion, and this for the reason that in neither case has Scott preserved the recited copies, if any, he made use of. The contention of Colonel Elliot is that he constructed the ballad of *Kinmont Willie* out of Scott of Satchell's rhyming *History of the Name of Scott* ; but although, in 1888, Mr Lang anticipated Colonel Elliot in at least hinting at this possibility, his opinion now is that there was a traditional ballad known to both. To say the least this is a possible, and it seems even a probable, supposition. Scott may have here and there got help from his namesake's *History*, but one can hardly doubt his good faith in writing, " This ballad is preserved by tradition on the West Borders, but much mangled by reciters." One can scarcely credit that in such a case he would state what was utterly untrue. But the strange fact remains that, mangled though these versions may have been, the ballad, as recorded by Scott, is the most perfect of all the Border ballads ; and of his method of making it so, this is all he tells us : " Some conjectural emendations have been absolutely necessary to render it intelligible " ; and he cites as an instance the substitution of the Eske for the Eden. Evidently, however, much more than " some conjectural emendations " were necessary to make it the splendid recital that it is ; and this is freely, if not fully enough, admitted by Mr Lang. His substantial contention is that while Scott may have made some use of the rhyming *History*, he had also other material, and did not forge, as Colonel Elliot contends, an entirely new Border ballad. Nevertheless it seems wellnigh certain that Scott's alterations and additions were so many and so important, that if he got the skeleton of the ballad from recital, he breathed the breath of life into what was practically dead, and a higher kind of life than it could have previously possessed.

In the case of *Jamie Telfer*, Mr Lang, while of opinion that there never was any such person, is disposed to believe in the true authenticity of Scott's version and to assign it priority over the

Elliot one (for which alone there is any MS. authority),
(1) because it is incredible that Scott of Buccleugh
would decline to help a spoiled Borderer, Jamie
Telfer or another, and (2) because the Scott version
is topographically the more correct of the two.   I
do not quite follow the argument of Mr Lang for
the non-existence of Jamie Telfer ; he might have
been a tenant in some lands of Dodhead, though
that property was possessed by the Scotts of
Satchell, or there might have been more than one
Dodhead, or the balladist or blundering tradition
might have given him the wrong farm.   While,
also, Mr Lang seems to dispose of Colonel Elliot's
argument that the Elliot version is topographically
the more correct, evidently this is of minor moment
if the ballad, as Mr Lang contends, be quite unhistorical ; and, indeed, the greater topographical
correctness of Scott's version might be due to
himself.   Mr Lang, adopting the opinion of Colonel
Elliot that the allegation that old Buccleugh refused
to help Telfer is " too absurd to be believed,"
points out that if it be, as Colonel Elliot thinks,
a later interpolation, this disposes of the Elliot
version, the narrative of which is wholly dependent
on Buccleugh's refusal.   But is the supposition so
absurd as both assert ?   In 1597, Buccleugh, for his
share in the Kinmont adventure, was induced to
enter into ward in England until he found pledges

for the maintenance of peace on the Borders. We may well believe that the arrangement brought him into bad odour with the Scottish Borderers ; and it would also make it impossible for him to grant them aid, if they brought an attack upon themselves. Thus the ballad, if founded more on fancy than fact, might well be intended as a skit on Buccleugh ; or it might even chronicle, however incorrectly in details, an actual case of a refusal of Buccleugh to grant aid to attacked Scottish Borderers. But apart from this, supposing the Elliot version were the only one known to Scott—and there is not convincing proof that he knew any other versions than Elliot ones—he could hardly resist removing from the ballad what he might well deem an unjust reflection on the head of his clan. Indeed one has difficulty in believing in the possibility of his giving the Elliot version a place in the *Minstrelsy* ; and it is a significant fact that though informed by Hogg that Hogg's mother's version of *Jamie Telfer* differed in many particulars from that in the *Minstrelsy*, he displayed no desire to obtain further information about the particulars from Hogg or a copy of his mother's version, which might, for anything Hogg stated, have been a Scott version, supposing a Scott version existed anywhere except in Sir Walter's own copy.

Several of the Scottish non-Border ballads are excel-

lent—some exceptionally excellent, productions.   A
version of *Captain Car* or *Edom o' Gordon* (178),
narrating the savage incidents attending the
burning of the House of Towie in Aberdeenshire in
1511, exists in the Cottonian MS. of not later date
than the end of the century.   It is an English reading
of a Scottish ballad, but a wonderfully good version,
and notable for a curious refrain representing the
desperate plight of Captain Car and his men on the
winter night, when they " must go take a hold " :—

> " Syck, sike, and to-towe sike,
>   And sike and like to die ;
>   The sikest nighte that euer I abode,
>   God lord haue mercy on me ! "

But this version cannot compare with the *Edom
o' Gordon* one, printed by Robert and Andrew Foulis
in 1755, from a copy supplied by Sir David Dalrymple
as " preserved in the memory of a lady," which,
whether a fake or not, is both ballad-like and
worthy, in certain stanzas, to rank with the greatest
achievements in descriptive verse.   In all ballad
literature it would be hard to find anything more
masterly in expression, more vividly graphic, or
more poignantly pathetic than the five stanzas
beginning :—

> " They row'd her in a pair of sheets,
>   And tow'd her ower the wa' ;
>   But on the point of Edom's spear
>   She gat a deadly fa'."

Were *Edom o' Gordon*, *Edward*, and *Sir Patrick Spens* (58) the work of the same balladist or fakist ? They well might be either the one or the other, but whoever made them what they are — what *Sir Patrick Spens* even must have been to be what it is as recorded in the Herd MS.—was, either as original creator or amender, a poetic artist in some respects as exceptional as Burns himself. Child has surmised that originally the Patrick Spens, or whatever his name might be, of this fine ballad may have been " only a shipmaster of purely local fame." Apparently the only reason for the surmise is the presence in these latter days of a ballad in Aberdeenshire termed *Young Allan* (245), which can hardly be aught else than a stupid travesty of *Sir Patrick Spens*. The skippers neither of " bonny Lothem," nor any other fishing village of the North of Scotland, were accustomed to sit " at the wine," or possess hawks or hounds or " gay ladys " ; nor could fishing cobbles, or even coasting schooners, carry " four-and-twenty feather beds " ; nor are there any other Scottish ballads which can reasonably be ascribed to the bards of the fishing villages ; nor is merely local fame a sufficient title to ballad celebration, unless the personages be of some rank.

Some of the later Scottish ballads detail domestic tragedies with a grim realism that is not ineffective.

In *The Laird of Wariston* (194) the steps of a sordid
tragedy are recounted with a certain sententious
succinctness.   Here is a portrait of the ill-used wife
who became the murderess of the laird :—

> " Down by yon garden green
>   Sae merrily as she gaes ;
> She has twa weel-made feet,
>   And she trips upon her taes.
>
> She has twa weel-made feet,
>   Far better is her hand ;
> She's as jimp in the middle
>   As any willow-wand."

The Baron of Brackley (203), with all the defective
rhymes in the versions that survive, is a splendid
sketch of Highland savagery and a wicked wife's
treachery.   The metre is peculiarly expressive of
the wild scene :—

> " Inverey cam doun Deeside, whistlin' and playin',
>   He was at brave Braikley's yett ere it was dawin'.
>
> He rappit fou loudly an' wi' a great roar,
>   Cried, ' Cum doun, cum doun, Braikley, and open the door.'
>
> Are ye sleepin', Baroune, or are ye wakin' ?
>   There's sharpe swords at your yett will gar your blood spin.' "

The final stanzas afford us a glimpse of the false
" pretty Pegg," the cause of the tragedy, " rantin'
and dancin' and singin' for joy ; " and the ballad
concludes with laconic brevity :—

" Ther's dool i' the kitchin and mirth i' the ha' :
    The Baroune o' Brackly is dead and awa'."

A somewhat different story of a woman's treachery
is *Sir James the Rose* (213), which seems to have
been greatly spoiled by the broadsidist.   A more
pleasing wife's tale is recorded in *Geordie* (209) ;
and there are some good elopement ballads, among
the best being *Bonny Baby Livingstone* (222) and
Jock o' Hazelgreen (293).

Such humorous tales as *The Jolly Beggar* (279),
Our Goodman (274), and *Get up and bar the Door*
(274), are, like *The Gaberlunzie Man*, productions
of clever, though unknown versifiers, probably
belonging to the Scottish gentry, and though, for
certain reasons, included in Child's collection,
no more accord with his conceptions of the ballad
than does, for example, *The Wife of Auchtermychty*
of the Bannatyne MS., or *Rob's Jock cam to woo our
Jenny*.   The later ballads dealing with the Covenant-
ing struggle—*Bothwell Bridge, Louden Hill, Philip-
haugh*, etc.—are of interest only as illustrative of
the decadence of the ballad art.   The semi-paganism
that had cradled the infancy of the earlier ballads
had long ceased to leave traces of its influence on
the imagination of the balladist ; the lot of the
minstrel also had long fallen on evil days, and
he had been superseded by the hack balladist and

the ragged ballad singer ; ballads, fallen from their
high estate, were preserved, now, mainly in the
confused memories of the lower classes ; feudalism
had vanished, and the conditions of society had
completely changed ; England had become a hum-
drum land of peace and plenty ; in Scotland the
ancient Border raids had ceased, and the Highland
system with its feuds and outrages had become
little more than a memory ; the age of machinery
had dawned ; the printing-press had superseded
recital ; and the ballad art, which, after some generations of decadency had in its old form hopelessly
perished, had begun to be cultivated, in a new
fashion, by the poets of the romantic revival.
Its later fortunes are, however, outside the scope of
the present volume.

SOME AUTHORITIES

English and Scottish Ballads, ed. F. J. Child, 5 vols., 1882-98 ; popular edit., with introd. by Professor Kittredge, in one vol., 1904.

Danmark's Gamle Folkeviser, ed. Svend Grundtvig, 5 vols., 1853-1890 ; continued by Dr Axel Olrik, as *Danske Ridderviser*, 1895, etc.

Alte Hoch und Nieder Deutsche Volkslieder, ed. J. H. Uhland, 1844-5.

H. Thuren, *Folke Sangen paa Færøerne*, 1908.

C. Nigra, *Canti popolari del Piemonte*, 1888.

Alfred Jeanroy, *Les Origines de la Poésie lyrique en France au moyen Age*, 1889.

Gaston Paris, *La Poésie du moyen Age*, 2 vols., 1885-1895, and various articles in *Romania* and the *Journal des Savants*.

Dr Axel Olrik, *Danske Folkeviser i Udvalg*, 1899.

L. Pineau, *Les Vieux Chants Populaires Scandinaves*, 1898.

G. Heusler, *Lied und Epos*, 1905.

Gérard du Nerval, *Chansons et Ballads populaire du Valois*, 1885.

C. Bücher, *Arbeit und Rhythmus*, 1909.

Percy Folio MS., ed. Hales and Furnival, 3 vols., 1867-8.

Sir Walter Scott's *Minstrelsy of the Scottish Border*, ed. T. F. Henderson, 4 vols., 1902.

Old English Ballads, ed. Professor F. B. Gummere, 1903.

Popular Ballads of the Olden Time, selected by Frank Sidgwick, 1903.

Professor W. P. Ker, *Epic and Romance*, 1897 ; and articles on the " Danish Ballads " in the *Scottish Historical Review* for July 1904 and July 1908.

Professor F. B. Gummere, *The Beginnings of Poetry*, 1901 ; *The Popular Ballad*, 1907 ; and article on the " Ballad " in the *Cambridge History of English Literature*, vol. ii.

Professor W. J. Courthope, *History of English Poetry*, vol. i., 1895.

Professor G. Gregory Smith, *The Transition Period*, 1900.

Col. F. Elliot, *Trustworthiness of the Border Ballads*, 1906 ; and *Further Essays on Border Ballads*, 1910.

Andrew Lang, *Sir Walter Scott and the Border Minstrelsy*, 1910; and article on the " Ballad " in *Chambers' Cyclopædia of English Literature*, 1902, and in *Encyclopædia Britannica*, 1910.

124

INDEX